THE MAGIC LANTERN

A Fable About Leadership, Personal Excellence and Empowerment

by Dr. Joe Rubino

The Magic Lantern:
A Fable About Leadership, Personal Excellence
and Empowerment
Dr. Joe Rubino

All enquiries regarding this publication to:-

Catalyst Books
13 New Row
Covent Garden, London
WC2N 4LF
Tel: 0207 380 4646
Fax: 0207 380 4647

www.catalystbooks.com

Printed by Redwood Books, Trowbridge, Wiltshire.

LCCN: 00-190587
ISBN: 0-9678529-3-5 CB

LCCN: 00-190587
ISBN: 0-9678529-0-0 PB

Dedication

For Amanda, Tommy, Nick and Anna

"*Leadership is the most pivotal and important profession of this millennium. The new leaders of society will take it on as a learned skill, identifying themselves as professional leaders capable of leading people in any "do the right thing" endeavor. Dr. Joe Rubino is one of these new professional leaders. This fable is an extraordinarily powerful window to experience this new leadership distinction.*

— Richard Bliss Brooke
Author, *Mach II With Your Hair on Fire*

"The Magic Lantern *is a true gift of love and light to the world. Inspirationally moving and wonderfully entertaining, it's a magical tale about an unstoppable commitment to leadership, personal development and impacting others to be happy, effective and powerful. Take on the lessons it conveys and you'll make a great difference in the lives you'll touch and in your own life as well.*"

— Cynthia Kersey
Author, *Unstoppable*

"*You'll have to decide for yourself if Joe Rubino is a modern day Tolkien and* The Magic Lantern *is an enlightened* Hobbit. *I do know that you'll enjoy your journey with Jake, Hunter, Nilrem and all the rest. And you'll learn a lot along the way. Have fun and learn. What a concept. Thanks Joe!*"

— John Milton Fogg
Author, *The Greatest Networker in the World*

The Magic Lantern *is a wonderfully fun, enchanting and brilliant book. It is a must for people of all ages who aspire to be the best they can be while striving for personal excellence, leadership and a life that works. Follow the principles that Dr. Joe brings to life with this delightful tale and you will be well on your way to a happier, more productive, successful and fulfilling life.*

— Jan Ruhe
Author, *Fire Up!*

"Dr. Joe Rubino, the master of success principles, has spun a delightful, inspirational, and wisdom packed parable as a gift to the human race. Learn the seven keys to unlocking the door to your success. Apply them and you'll change your life . . . and quite possibly your world!"

— Bob Burg
Author, *Endless Referrals* and
Winning Without Intimidation

"The Magic Lantern is a masterful blend of Richard Bach's Illusions *and Tolkien's* The Hobbit. *The seven key self-discovery and leadership principles are easy to read, impactful, and possibly even life changing."*

— Brian Klemmer
Author, *If How To's Were Enough,*
We Would All be Skinny, Rich and Happy

Contents

Acknowledgment

Special thanks go to my mentors, Mike Smith, Carol McCall and Richard Brooke. These three people have contributed enormously to the personal development conversation that will be the primary focus of the true leaders of the new millennium. Smith and McCall are champions of personal empowerment, while Brooke is a true visionary responsible for developing tens of thousands of "do the right thing" leaders.

All three daily teach the concepts outlined in this fable with great impact. They have personally helped me to discover "what I didn't know I didn't know" about myself and others while inspiring me to make the most of what I did know.

Special thanks also go to my two partners in life.

The Magic Lantern

First, to my wife, Janice, whose tremendous support allows me to pursue my passions of personal empowerment and leadership development. For that I am truly grateful. Also, sincere thanks to Dr. Tom Ventullo, my lifelong friend and business partner who shares my commitment to impact the world through our two companies, The Center For Personal Reinvention and Visionary International Partnerships. It is through his unselfish commitment to the excellence of all people that our work is able to reach the hearts of many. Thank you for sharing your gifts of listening and coaching with the world.

A special acknowledgement to Marianne Williamson for sourcing the quote at the end of Chapter 11. It was adapted from her quotation, "Our deepest fear is not that we are inadequate. Our deepest fear is that we are powerful beyond measure."

Thanks also to Beki Thacker and Tom Bellucci for their technical support and Evelyn Howell, my editor, for helping make this book a reality.

To all of these extraordinary individuals and to you, the reader, may the Magic Lantern's eternal flame burn forever in your hearts so that this work might continue to impact millions and, in doing so, change the world.

The Magic Lantern

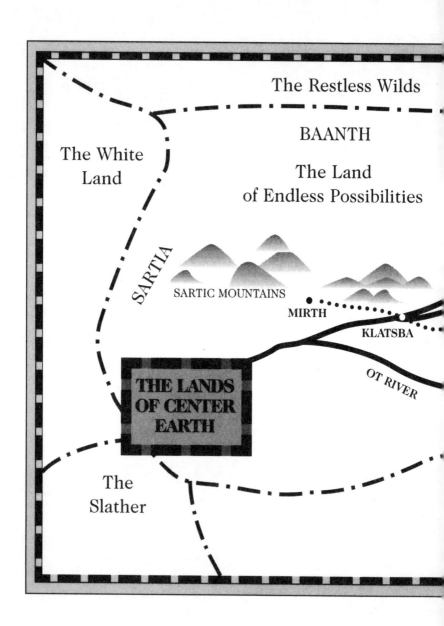

The Restless Wilds

BAANTH

The Land
of Endless Possibilities

The White
Land

SARTIA

SARTIC MOUNTAINS

MIRTH

KLATSBA

OT RIVER

THE LANDS
OF CENTER
EARTH

The
Slather

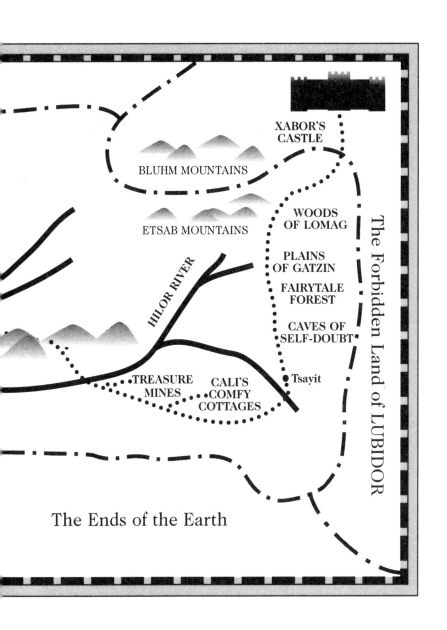

XABOR'S
CASTLE

BLUHM MOUNTAINS

ETSAB MOUNTAINS

WOODS
OF LOMAG

PLAINS
OF GATZIN

FAIRYTALE
FOREST

CAVES OF
SELF-DOUBT

HILOR RIVER

TREASURE
MINES

CALI'S
COMFY
COTTAGES

Tsayit

The Forbidden Land of LUBIDOR

The Ends of the Earth

The Magic Lantern

Chapter

The Crystal Cave

I n the White Mountains of rural New Hampshire, there lived a decent, law-abiding, downright ordinary family named the Jilians. The family was headed up by Chip, a jack-of-all-trades and master of none — as he would refer to himself — and his wife, Sarah. Chip was the spitting image of his dad. (God rest his soul.) Folks told him so all the time. And this wasn't exactly a compliment — if you get my meaning. He was a large man, tipping the scale at about 380. Chip had a round red face, curly brown thinning hair, no neck to speak of and a bushy multicolored beard that hadn't seen a trimmer since who knows when. His thick, black-rimmed glasses were a couple of sizes too small for his face, so they dug into his ample skin, leaving a permanent indentation on each side of his head. When he walked, he waddled from side to side like a duck that has an equilibrium problem, his ample rear-end knocking things over as he went. Chip worked for the local Wentworth golf course in Jackson, doing odd jobs and a little of whatever needed to be done. The truth be told, they were usually the lousy, dirty jobs no one else wanted. Everybody at Wentworth knew that when you have a smelly, rotten chore like cleaning out the pigs' pen at the kiddie petting zoo or a heavy, backbreaking task like building the boulder wall around Green #17, just call old Chipper! He'll do it — like it or not.

It had become the local joke: "What can we stick Chip with today?" Some said Chip must not be too bright. Others thought he was afraid to speak up for himself and turn down these "doozie jobs," as he called them. Neither was true. Chip just felt lucky, in a way, to have any old job at all — thinking of himself as he did. But, deep down, it really did tick him off.

Sarah was the "brains" of the family — at least according to Chip. She was what folks called a "plain" girl when they wanted to be nice. A wave of brown hair covered her watery gray eyes, which hid behind catlike spectacles. Her badly crowded smile was the focal point people noticed in conversation even though they pretended not to look. No matter what folks thought, Sarah was the love of Chip's life and he was awfully happy to have her.

Sarah worked at the local Wal-Mart three days a week as a cashier and at home making curtains and doing clothing alterations for local folks the rest of the time. These odd jobs allowed her to spend more time with the Jillian's only son, 15-year-old Jake. Sarah was a *great* mom. On that everyone agreed. From the time Jake was an infant, she spent every possible opportunity teaching her son all there was to know about the world and its people — and how to be most effective with both.

The Jilians lived in a tiny three-room log cabin set off a dirt road on Christmas Mountain, on the edge of the White Mountain National Forest. It was in that very cabin that Chip's folks and their folks before them had lived. Sure, it had been spruced up and modernized a bit over the years, but it was a pretty humble abode nonetheless — complete with the Jilian's old 1968 Frigidaire still in the front yard. Sarah had tried to get Chip to haul the old eyesore away for the longest time, but it never quite made that day's priority list. Judging from the looks of the Jilian place and the rusting '75 Chevy truck parked out front, most people may have considered the Jilians poor. But not them. They focused on the rugged mountain beauty that surrounded them instead of what Chip called that "highfalutin city-slicker stuff." Sarah was fond of saying, "If you've got to be poor, you might as well be poor in the mountains of New Hampshire rather than the streets of New York City."

Jake was Chip and Sarah's pride and joy. Folks joked about how Chip could have such a normal son. They gave Sarah all the credit here. At 15, Jake sported an athlete's build. No Chip Jilian rear-end genes here! Jake was smart as they come and wise beyond his years. All his teachers said so — even his English teacher, Mrs. Pratz, who thought they didn't make gifted kids any more. He was a straight-A honor student all right. The only worry his parents had about Jake was he tended to be a loner. Folks said he hung around with that dog of his maybe a bit too much. In Jake, Chip and Sarah saw their hope for the future. Like all parents, they wanted the best for their son. They would often tell Jake just how proud they were of him and how, someday, he would go off, leaving their little backwoods home and make his mark in the world. Jake appreciated his parents' confidence in him, but their constant reminders that he would, one day, make a difference put a lot of pressure on him. He worried a lot about how he might be able to live up to their dreams.

One of Jake's favorite pastimes was taking long walks in the woods with his faithful dog, Hunter — a beautiful yellow Labrador retriever. Since the day four years ago when Jake had found Hunter as a starving puppy caught in a hunter's trap, the two had been inseparable friends. Jake and Hunter would often take long walks together in the woods. All the while, Jake would contemplate just how he might grow up to realize his folks' high expectations.

Jake collected rocks and fossils and crystals. His room was crammed with odd stones he couldn't resist picking up. One of Jake's favorite places to go to dream was an old cave located about halfway up the mountain side, a little way off the hiking trail behind the Jilian home. This cave led to an abandoned tin mine that had been closed down and boarded up in the early 1800s. Jake would hike up to the cave with his dog and his flashlight, always finding more and more interesting rocks and crystals to add to his mushrooming collection.

Jake had hiked up this mountain with his dad ever since he was four years old — just as Chip's dad had done with him when Chip was a little boy. You see,

Chip could not bear the thought that he was weak and he was going to make darn sure that Jake would not grow up to be weak either. As a matter of fact, he got his nickname as a boy from constantly getting into one fight after another to prove that he was tough. The kids started to call him "Chip" because of the huge "chip on his shoulder" as he picked fight after fight. And the name just stuck.

Chip Jilian believed in always stretching his son and challenging him to be the best he could be. Jake often wondered why his dad wasn't nearly as demanding when it came to himself. Early on, Chip would make the little boy lead the way up the mountain trail, reminding him all the way that he could make it — if he thought he could. Any time little Jake slowed down and complained that he was getting tired, Chip would say, "Stop your whining, Jake. You can make it. Hurry up or I'll leave you behind."

For a four-year-old, the thought of being left behind on a mountain trail was terrifying. His legs might ache and his heel might be blistered, but then and there Jake decided that he would do whatever it takes to reach the top and not be left behind. He also decided that to please his dad and not have him leave him, Jake would need to be strong, unemotional and committed to achieving his goals — no matter what. The last time Jake cried was when he was four years old.

Now, at the age of 15, despite his father's warnings to keep away from it, the old cave had become a retreat for Jake to visit any time he needed to think, deal with life's challenges or contemplate just how he would make his mark on the world. He named his favorite retreat "The Crystal Cave," not only for the wide variety of crystal formations he discovered there but also because the cave helped him to become "crystal clear" about whatever he was contemplating at any particular time.

One very fine, bright autumn day, when all the magnificent fall foliage colors of yellow, red and orange were at their spectacular peak throughout the White Mountains, Jake and Hunter decided to hike to the Crystal Cave to think and explore. Each time Jake explored the dozens of winding tunnels that led deep within the cave's secret inner-most reaches, he would uncover new and interesting passages and rock formations. All the while, he was also discovering new truths. Every time Jake would discover a new insight about himself or about life and people in general, he would write his discovery on the cave walls with brightly colored permanent markers, much like our cave dweller ancestors did with their mineral pigments thousands of years ago.

Jake could readily recognize the passages he had explored already by reading his insights on the passage walls. On this crisp fall day as he entered a tunnel, on his right he read,

"Knowledge is power."

His mom often repeated this phrase as she encouraged him to pursue the education she and Chip had missed. It was on the day that Jake wrote that phrase that he decided that he would certainly attend college and become the first in his family with a formal education.

Jake and Hunter pushed deeper into the bowels of the next tunnel. Jake shone his flashlight on another quote he had inscribed on the wall,

"All of our dreams can come true if we have the courage to pursue them."

Jake took this quote from Walt Disney. In school, he had learned of Disney's dream to create a land where both kids and adults could play, dream and stay young at heart their whole lives through. He longed to one day visit Disney World and to create something of comparable magnitude himself as his gift to the world. Now as he passed Walt's words, Cinderella's Castle appeared before his mind's eye. He saw the poor, mistreated girl go from her rags and ashes to attend the ball and meet her prince. Jake turned to Hunter and said, "I wonder when my dreams will come true. I can feel it's going to be soon."

Suddenly, a bat swooped down missing his head by inches. He lunged back in fright, nearly trampling Hunter in the process. As he stepped down into the sunken recess of the next passage, he noticed yet another inscription on the cave wall,

"Love keeps the heart forever young."

This, too, was one of his mom's favorites — one she would repeat to Jake each night before bedtime as she wished him pleasant dreams. Love was clearly the secret to both health and happiness he decided. "But why don't most people 'get it'?" he yelled at Hunter.

Upon entering another of the cave's tunnels, Jake realized that his familiar markings were absent from the walls of this new passage. Excited about what lay

The Magic Lantern

ahead and fueled by his desire to explore new and undiscovered realms of the cave, he continued further into the cave's remote reaches. Jake could see signs that tin miners had long ago preceded him, leaving a broken pick ax here and a rusted pail there.

As he and Hunter reached the far end of the tunnel, it appeared that they could go no further. Jake was suddenly inspired to write on the wall in big red letters a quote by T.S. Eliot,

> *"ONLY those who risk going too far can possibly find out how far one can go."*

His intuition told him that danger lay ahead, but he decided to ignore it. The lure of new discoveries in uncharted territory was too great for him to resist. Jake would soon learn that his intuition was never wrong. Whenever he chose to dismiss it, a new lesson reminding him of its accuracy awaited.

Jake surveyed the situation. Thick oak logs and stones loosely piled one on top of another blocked their way from floor to ceiling. Undaunted, Jake began to pry at one of the wedged logs with an old pick ax he found there. Using the ax handle as a lever, he managed to pry one of the logs loose. The opening was just wide enough for Hunter and him to squirm through. "We did it, boy," he shouted in delight. As Hunter squeezed by Jake into the mine shaft, he brushed against his arm, forcing Jake to drop the flashlight. It hit the ground with a thud, causing the chamber to fill with blackness.

"Now you've done it, Hunter!" Jake scolded. "You've broken our flashlight, and it's pitch dark in here!" In the dark, Jake became easily disoriented, not knowing which way led out to the passageway through the crack they had created in the rock and log wall. He grabbed hold of Hunter's collar and with one hand on the wall, slowly felt his way along in search of the elusive opening. Jake could hear his father's words echo clearly in his mind, "You made your bed, now lie in it." He knew that he had to be strong and keep his senses, even though the little boy in him wanted to sit down and cry.

Just as Jake took his fifth step along the perimeter of the wall, he felt himself lose his footing. Before he knew it, he and Hunter were in a free fall, tumbling straight down for what seemed like an eternity. All Jake could think of as he feared for his life was his dad warning him to stay out of that cave.

The Magic Lantern

Chapter 2

The Land
of Endless
Possibilities

When Jake opened his eyes, he found himself staring up at Hunter. His best friend was licking his face while excitedly wagging his tail. Dizzily, Jake sat up and looked left and right. He was lying in a huge field of dense flowers of every shape and color. Never before had he witnessed such a dazzling blend of vivid reds, yellows, blues and lavenders. How strange it seemed that he should find himself in such a beautiful and colorful setting when, moments before, he was in a dark and lifeless mine shaft. As Jake jumped to his feet, he noticed a large billboard flanking the cobblestone road that ran its way through the field of flowers. The billboard read in large colorful letters,

The Magic Lantern

"Welcome Home, Jake Jilian.
We've Been Expecting You!"

How bizarre, Jake thought. "Welcome home? Why, I'm not home at all." As he had this thought, he turned around to hear a chorus chant in unison,

Hooray, hooray, he's here at last
From lands of far and tales of past.
The scrolls of old have come to be.
The boy we've sought will set us free!

We've waited long
For wars to cease,
To show us how
To live in peace,
To break the pattern
We've all known,
The boy king's here
To claim his throne!

With a puzzled expression, Jake looked at Hunter and said, "There must be some mistake."

Just then a small dwarf emerged from behind a row of tall sunflower plants. The dwarf was about four feet tall. He wore a floppy red cap and sported a long curly red beard. His blue smock was neatly tucked into a pair of brown-green knickers held up by a pair of solid gold suspenders that outlined his prominently protruding belly.

"Why, who are you?" Jake blurted out in startled disbelief.

"I'm Nilrem the Knowing, your guide here in the Land of Endless Possibilities."

"You're who? In the Land of What?" Jake thought he must surely have lost his mind.

"Welcome, my lord Jake. Please permit me to explain. According to dwarfen legend, Center Earth was formed some 24,000 years ago with the rising and falling of lands above in the world of men. In the land your people call Atlantis, there came to be a major cataclysm. Technology had advanced to the stage where it was possible to harness the sun's power through crystals. For many years, such power was harnessed for the good of the people. Your ancient cities relied upon this energy source for many noble uses — to heat and cool your homes, power your vehicles both on the land and in the air and heal the sick. As with any creation, the crystals were neither good nor bad in and of themselves. They could be used for either good or evil purpose. Just as there were many who utilized these tools for the service of man, there were many who sought to use them to satisfy their greed for power and wealth."

Jake listened, dumbfounded, as Nilrem continued the story. "These ill-directed leaders of Atlantis had applied these solar powered energy sources to the splitting of atoms with the intention to use such tools as weapons of mass destruction. During one such test deep beneath the earth's crust, they were unable to control the awesome magnitude of energy that had been generated. This energy was released too near a fault line. The result was the event known in Jake's world as the Great Flood. The north and south poles shifted. Previously dry lands sank and were inundated with water. Lands formerly buried deep below the ocean surface rose.

"At the same time, far beneath the earth's surface," Nilrem said, "some of the fault lines widened from the blast. An atmosphere was created deep within the planet itself and our world, Center Earth was born. Over the next thousand years or so, the radiation from the explosion in the world above reached the life forms that were taking hold here in our world, causing some severe mutations in the root races. The result was the creation of such groups we know here as dwarves, elves, fairies, goblins, gnomes, orcs and trolls, to name just a few.

"Over the next thousand years there was great chaos. The members of the various races multiplied and there was competition for land, food and natural resources. War and enormous turmoil resulted. There was much loss of life and division in the land.

"Among the different races, several leaders emerged. One such dwarfen leader was King Wiggen, the wise. He convened a council comprised of leaders from every race and territory with the intention of restoring peace and cooperation in Center Earth. He was successful and the peace he established would endure for more than three thousand years.

"Wiggen was both a visionary ruler and gifted wizard and seer. He predicted that in Center Earth's future, there would be periods of harmony followed by periods of discord for ages to come. He saw the rise of benevolent leaders of each race alternating with the rise of weak and cruel tyrants. He documented these predictions, naming the many good and evil leaders that were to come. These prophesies were written in a series of scrolls found hidden many generations ago in caves in the region we call the Restless Wilds. These predictions have indeed come to pass throughout our history.

"Wiggen further promised a time would come when he would return to Center Earth, long after his death, to restore peace and tranquility to a troubled world. He said he would come from the world above as a boy named Jake Jilian. It is so written in our scrolls."

Jake was astounded. "How could this be?" he mumbled, half to himself.

"We're the answer to your prayers and you're the answer to ours!" the little man continued.

And as he spoke these words, hundreds of other dwarves dressed in every color of the rainbow popped out from their hiding places and continued to sing their welcome chant:

He's traveled long from places dank,
Where hammers swung and picks once clanked.
To leave his mark in the world above,
He first must learn to share his love.

Nilrem continued in his curiously high-pitched voice, "You wished to learn the secrets that would allow you to impact the world. We are here to lead you to those discoveries. And you are here to lead us too. Have no fear. After all, we are only here by your design to fulfill the prophecies of old."

"By my design? Are you crazy?" Jake said, still in shock. "Why, I've never met any of you before, and I certainly don't remember anything about any King Wiggen. I had an accident, and I just want to go home. Can you help me do that? And, by the way, where exactly am I again?"

"Please trust us, Jake. All of life is a coming home, and there are no accidents," Nilrem replied. "Even when you may find yourself lost and on a dark path, you possess inside the power to light your way. We are responsible for everything that shows up around us in life. We attract everything — health or illness, wealth or poverty, happiness or sorrow. The sooner we realize this, the sooner we can create the things we know will really support us. You, my friend, whether you remember it or not, are in the Land Of Endless Possibilities. And, yes, I can help you find the way 'home' — but first we've got some work to do. Now, kindly follow me."

Just as Nilrem spoke these words, a small red hummingbird not much larger than a bumblebee

swooped down and hovered above his shoulder. The
hummingbird spoke to Nilrem in frantic, staccato
bursts. "Oh, great Nilrem the Knowing! You must
come! Quickly! Chaos! In the village! There is more
talk of war! The elders await! The boy's arrival! The
day which was prophesied! In the sacred scrolls of
long ago! Found in the caves of the Restless Wilds. Is
now come to pass!"

Jake signaled Hunter that it was all right, deciding
to trust the process. With great urgency, they followed
Nilrem and the many dwarves out of the field of flowers and into the adjacent woods. After about an hour's
brisk jog on a well-worn and crooked path surrounded by thousand-year-old giant sequoia trees, they
emerged into a clearing that marked the outskirts of
the village. Jake could see crowds of angry little people standing in the square. There were arguments
everywhere. Some were shouting, others crying, others actually pummeled their fellows with fists and
clubs. Still others were angrily complaining about the
dreadful fighting that was to come. Some were even
cowering behind carts and fences, obviously trying to
hide because they feared what might happen to them
if they were to come out. Disharmony was everywhere.

The Magic Lantern

"Why is everyone so angry and upset?" Jake asked. "The council of elders expects you in the town hall. There you will learn more," Nilrem assured him. Nilrem led Jake through a large hole in the ground under the roots of a stately old oak tree. They descended into a great and ornately decorated underground hall that had once been built by an ancient race of dwarves who had originally occupied the area many, many years ago. The current occupants used the hall to entertain special guests of larger stature who would not fit comfortably into their usual underground holes. They proceeded down some squeaking wooden stairs and passed through the arched oaken doorway to the high council chamber.

At an oblong cherry table with carved lions feet were seated the nine distinguished town elders. The eldest dwarf and the council's spokesperson was Traylor.

Nearly four feet 10 inches tall, he was the tallest of his village. Traylor was dressed in a distinguished royal blue cape with ruffled shirt and held a black riding stick in hand. He was proud to be the only dwarf in the entire village tall enough to ride on horseback. He appeared to represent all that was cultured and refined in dwarfdom.

The Magic Lantern

The Land of Endless Possibilities

As Nilrem and Jake entered the room, Traylor raised his arms, beckoning the remaining eight elders to rise in unison and bow a welcoming greeting to their esteemed and expected guest.

"On behalf of the council of elders and the village of Mirth in the Land Of Endless Possibilities, I welcome you, Lord Jake. Your arrival on this very day was foretold in our sacred scrolls handed down to us from generation to generation since the time of their discovery. Allow me to introduce our respected council members. From the region of Baanth in the north, I present Yint, Trilion and Vester."

Yint and Trilion were brothers and Vester was their cousin. All three were dressed in purple robes with matching berets and scarves, as was the custom in Baanth. As his name was called, each new dwarf took one step forward, bowed politely and offered a gracious smile followed by a stern frown.

Jake was stumped by these apparently conflicting gestures. He looked at Nilrem in puzzlement. Nilrem whispered behind his hand, "Here in the Land of Endless Possibilities, we are very aware of the fact that opposites exist together in all realms of being. You can not be happy without knowing what it is like to be sad. You can not have good without evil. Up without down. Love without hate. To show one emotion without acknowledging its opposite emotion is considered hypocrisy by many dwarves from the old school! Their gestures are consistent with respecting this important truth."

Traylor continued, "From the Sartic Mountains in the west come Plitor, Rilia and Nargen."

Plitor was the youngest among the group of elders. He and Rilia had decided to follow Nargen's lead and venture out of the remote and primitive Mountains of Sartia to Mirth to be part of something grand. What that was, they did not know as yet. But they trusted Nargen, and Nargen said it would be special. And by orcs and ogres, that was enough for them!

Nargen knew from a very young age that he would be a great military leader one day. He had trained long and hard in the infamous jungles of The Slather to the south of Sartia in preparation for his military career. You simply would not believe the stories that came out of The Slather! Tales of hardship, courage and battles against insurmountable odds involving all sorts of wild creatures were the subject around many an evening's campfire. The Slather contained the stuff out of which legends were made. Nargen himself was a legend — at least in his own mind. He had been heavily decorated for bravery in dozens of battles and was a veteran of countless wars between the dwarves and most of their neighbors. He saw Plitor and Rilia as his protégées and had great hopes that they would one day distinguish themselves in battle as well.

Traylor continued, "From the line of Grebon in the river valley of Ot to the south come Wert and Shayli."

Though related somehow in their distant family lineage, Wert and Shayli could not have been less alike. Wert was an angry dwarf known for making up outrageous stuff in his head and then acting as though it were true. If there was a disruption going on, Wert was probably in the middle of it.

On the other hand, many saw Shayli as a wise and generous father figure. He proved time and again to be a stabilizing influence for not only Wert but all who knew him.

After each of the elders was introduced and each acknowledged their special guest in the same way, Traylor nodded his head, indicating that they were to be seated. Jake was offered the seat of honor at the table's north end, and Nilrem was guided to the seat at his right hand.

Jake was not quite sure what to make of his hosts.

Each of the dwarf elders seemed friendly enough, but in a strangely cantankerous sort of way.

"Can someone please tell me more about why I'm here and what else the scrolls say about expecting me?" Jake pleaded.

"Why, of course," responded Traylor, as he smiled and frowned in reply. "Please pardon our rudeness."

"In the days of old before the Magic Lantern was stolen from our midst, dwarves would travel from near and far to take up residence in the village of Mirth. For, you see, we had prospered in peace and love for well over a thousand years, bathed in the peaceful glow of the Magic Lantern's light. Then, one day, the evil sorcerer, Xabor, cast a spell of sleepiness over the entire village. While the village slept, he commanded his band of trolls to enter the village and steal the Magic Lantern. Before its theft, the lantern had cast its light of love and peace over all ever since it was hung in the square to mark the beginning of the thousand-year reign of peace of our good Queen Matilda."

"Ever since that day when the lantern vanished, the village of Mirth has become known as the village of Constant Upset instead," added Nilrem. "In this village, without the light of the Magic Lantern to light their way, the villagers are constantly at odds with each other, warring with their elf, goblin, orc and troll neighbors and unable to even get along with themselves and other dwarf factions."

"But how could a lantern make so much of a difference and result in so much upset, Nilrem?" Jake interjected.

"Without the Magic Lantern's light, the villagers are powerless to control their addiction to being right and making others wrong. Without the light of reason and an ability to recognize their destructive moods of anger, sadness and fear, they are at the whim of these moods. They live in constant conflict with everyone they meet. They sacrifice everything that they value just to be right. It seems that they are constantly in their very destructive moods! They have lost their ability to recognize when they are in these moods and manage them. Instead, they act continually from these emotions of anger, sadness and fear."

"But what can I do to help such a mess?" offered Jake.

Nilrem explained, "Ever since the days of old, long before the reign of King Wiggen, before the flood washed away all life except for our surviving ancestors, Esmerelda and Arbor, it has been prophesied that a great and wise leader from the world of men would come to save our dwarfen race."

With these words, he pulled from beneath his smock an old and tattered brown parchment scroll from which he read:

When all seems bleak
And marked by hate,
When the light of Matilda
Has left this gate

And dwarf fights dwarf
And troll and elf,
When hatred replaces
Love of self

And all that's heard
Are angry screams,
And the blood of villagers
Makes red the streams

From the darkened caves in the world of men
Will come a prince to restore hope again,
To return to Mirth the magic glow

The Magic Lantern

That lights the world
And soothes the soul.

Nilrem paused to see the elders nodding in approval, yes, then no — as was their custom. He continued,

To fetch the Light from Xabor's midst
Golden keys to seven locks must fit.

To win the keys, the prince must solve
The missing pieces to involve
What makes for man and dwarf and elf
To live in love and not for self.

The secrets come from tablets seven,
Strewn along the path to heaven.
The tablets' tales make wise the knowing
And return the magic light to glowing!

From his seat at the table, Shayli looked to Traylor for permission to speak. Traylor nodded his approval, and Shayli stood and bowed toward Jake, his long gray beard touching his misshapen feet.

The dwarves' learned scholar and chief historian, Shayli continued in a low and raspy voice, "The scrolls portend that you, Lord Jake, must find the seven keys and with them seven accompanying tablets as you make your way along the tortuous path to Xabor's castle. The keys are foretold to unlock the seven locks of the dungeon vault in the castle of the evil sorcerer. Here the Magic Lantern is hidden. You must travel through the Land of Endless Possibilities in search of the seven truths — written one on each tablet. Each truth will earn you a key. When you have learned these seven truths and gathered your seven keys, you will be able to then unlock the secret to peace and harmony held within the powers of the Magic Lantern. The future of all the world, both the lands of Center Earth here and those above in the world of men, depend upon your success."

General Nargen, bravest of all dwarf warriors, now stood. He bowed in honor of their guest and spoke. "Lord Jake, there will be many challenges that you will encounter on your quest for the seven golden keys. With your blessing, I shall assemble a company of dwarfen elite and battle-honed veteran warriors. These Longbeards shall be at your beck and call, ever ready to fight any goblin, troll, giant or other enemy that should cross our path. We stand ready to serve the dwarfen empire with our lives."

The Magic Lantern

Nargen let go a shrill whistle, and in an instant, two Hammerers entered, the fiercest of the dwarfen hand-picked bodyguards. With their elaborately crafted, jeweled double-handed hammers, they appeared ready to take on all enemies with an angry bludgeoning vengeance.

Jake surveyed the Longbeards and the Hammerers with a tip-to-toe glance. He shivered and broke out into a cold sweat. His heart told him that there had to be a better way to reclaim the Magic Lantern without the bloodshed that these fierce troops would bring. He thought about his dad and worried what he'd say when he learned of the pickle Jake had gotten himself into. He knew, surely, his mom would not approve. Nevertheless, he reluctantly agreed to have Nargen ready the troops — just in case.

Chapter

The Journey Begins

Troubled by the thought of the perilous journey that lay ahead, Jake and Hunter slept hardly a wink that night, tossing and turning in their four-foot-long dwarfen beds. At dawn's break, they were summoned by Yint and Vester and requested to join the war party in front of the statue of Graebek, the great dwarfen dragon slayer of old. Yint gave both Jake and Hunter two stale and rather tasteless seed cakes along with a flask of water before hurrying them on their way.

Already assembled in the town square were the members of the party charged with the lantern's safe return. Leading the group was Nargen, accompanied by his army of 18 battle-ready dwarfen warriors, 12 elite Longbeards and four fearsome Hammerers. They brought with them the most advanced war machines known to Center Earth: stone-throwing and fire-spewing cannons, devastating organ guns and, of course, war clubs and hammers for all.

Nilrem and the other elders followed them. None would think of passing up their chance to partake in the mission, counting on the fame it would bring. All relished the thought that future dwarfen ballads would tell of their bravery and sing their praises.

Nilrem instructed Plitor and Wert to oversee the distribution of provisions and supplies. Sacks of grains, loaves of bread and cakes of many varieties were divided up among the men. Wert also made sure that each dwarf received four large flasks of water to begin their journey. It would be a long trek across the Hilor River, through the Plains of Gatzin, past the Woods of Lomag and beyond the Etsab Mountains deep into the Forbidden Land of Lubidor, where Xabor's castle was hidden.

Jake was beginning to feel even more uneasy about what was to come. Fighting, killing, looting and seeking revenge were all that the dwarfen race seemed to know.

The Magic Lantern

The Journey Begins

How could he be a part of this fierce and vengeful band when all of the scrolls spoke of love and service to others? Perhaps, it would make more sense to him as things got underway. At least, he hoped it would.

That morning, the villagers were all out in droves to see their war party off. The angry quarreling, shouting and chaos of yesterday, the tears of sadness and fear of civil war were now temporarily replaced by a focused hatred of the evil Xabor and anyone else who should happen to get in the way of the dwarves' rightful return of the Magic Lantern. Jake overheard Yint remark to Wert, "There's nothing like a war to help focus people's hatred on a productive cause!"

So, to shouts of "Kill Xabor," "Off with trolls' heads," "Slay a dragon for me," and the like, the ornery troop marched off toward the direction of the river Hilor in search of their destiny. As the band departed, Hunter looked up at Jake as if to say, "Are you sure that you know what you're getting us into?"

The troop marched for eight straight days, making camp each night to rest for the next day and revel in the adventures they imagined to come. The Longbeards spoke of the glories of past wars and of wiping out entire elfin villages. The dwarfen warriors relished the day that they would experience the status of becoming revered Longbeards themselves. The elders spoke of how fortunate their village was to have in their midst such brave and ruthless warriors.

Jake listened to all the tales of gore and glory and wondered aloud how the conquered enemies must have felt.

At that moment, two dwarf scouts entered the camp, reporting that the elfin village of Klatsba lay just ahead at the junction between two wide rivers. The village was directly on the path that the dwarves must take to reach their destination in the Forbidden Land in search of the lantern.

This news was just what the dwarfen warriors wanted to hear. It was a chance to prove their bravery and re-ignite the dwarfen-elfin wars. In the process, they would, of course, unfortunately have to slaughter a lot of innocent elfin women and children — as must occur in all wars. Or, so they told themselves.

The dwarves rallied to the call and made ready for battle. They cared not that the elves were generally a peace-loving race and, at this time in history, not at war with the dwarfen people.

After all, the dwarves were in pursuit of a noble cause — to return the Magic Lantern and restore harmony to their village. There was only one route

The Journey Begins
_____

leading in the direction that they must travel and that
elfin village was right smack-dab in the way.

Throughout the troop, rationalization after rationalization was offered to justify the forthcoming
slaughter. It wasn't the dwarves' fault that the elves
happened to build their village there. Past wars had
resulted in dwarves and elves becoming naturally
sworn enemies. The dwarves had a right to protect
their own people and get to their destination as rap-
idly as was possible. This and similar logic could be
heard in the dwarfen camp as they made ready for
battle. Their mood had an angry, indignant flavor of
righteousness to it — as is necessary for any group to
declare war on another and feel good about it.

Jake was in a quandary. Somehow he felt responsible for this situation. On one hand, these people
were just acting out what had been foretold in the
ancient scrolls. But, at the same time, he couldn't just
sit back and watch a bloody, unnecessary war break
out. He closed his eyes as his mom had taught him in
times of need and prayed for help.

Just then, as if in answer to his prayers, a
bright light flashed before him. There stood a beautiful, dark-haired young woman in a flowing, white
gossamer gown.

The Magic Lantern
_____

"I am the white wizardess, Tonesia," she said. "I am here so that you might grow in your wisdom and be of service to others so that they might grow as well. My life purpose is to serve those who serve. As prophesied in the ancient scrolls, you have been chosen to lead these beings to the light of wisdom and love. I am here to help you in this role. And, for now, I am visible only to you."

Jake nearly fainted with surprise. When he recovered his composure, he smiled nervously at Tonesia and said, "Things appear to be out of control. There is great danger ahead, and a thirst for blood and revenge here. These dwarves look to me for guidance, and yet I know not how to guide them. I fear there will be terrible suffering and loss of life. How can you help us?"

Tonesia smiled lovingly at Jake and spoke, "The dwarves and the elves have been enemies for many years. Both people have known much suffering and loss of life. Each has used the love of hatred for each other to justify the repeated slaughters both sides have endured."

"So, how can we put an end to this madness?" Jake asked.

Tonesia's soulful brown eyes lit up. "The first law

of wisdom states, 'Act not in anger against others until you have first walked a mile in their shoes.'

"It is only by seeking to understand what it must be like in the other person's world that you can really appreciate your mutuality — that is, what you actually have in common with them. It is with this understanding of what it's like to actually be an elf that dwarves can then appreciate how their actions may affect others. Know that you have the power to make a difference here and always, all your days, no matter where you go. Know also that the love and wisdom you possess deep within your soul is there for you to call upon at will. Now, take this crystal amulet as a reminder of your awesome power to impact the world. Know as well that I will be with you always. You need only call my name in your hour of greatest need." And with those words, Tonesia disappeared.

Jake considered her words well and knew exactly what he had to do. He summoned Traylor and Nilrem and the rest of the elders and said, "What would it be like to be an elf sleeping in the village ahead? What if you were that elf with a loving wife and blessed children in your home? How would you feel if strangers came with clubs and hammers and cannons and slaughtered your loved ones just to make their passage through your village convenient for them and feed their lust for glory and fame?

"What if there was another peaceful way to not only make your way through the village but to create a new way of being for both elf and dwarf alike? If you were the little elf child, would you appreciate the dwarves considering the possibility that there might be a better way to make it through and leave others whole at the same time?"

The elders were taken aback. This perspective had never even remotely been considered by any of them. Plitor spoke first. "But what of fame and glory? What of the heroic battle stories that would go untold if war were avoided?"

Traylor responded, "What if new tales of wisdom and compassion were to replace those of blood and guts? What if a new era of peace meant that your own children would live to a ripe old age instead of being slaughtered by any of the self-proclaimed dwarfen enemies? Just maybe, if we decide to spare this village this time, they may, in turn, put themselves in our shoes, and spare our village the next."

"That's a good point," offered Wert. "One I hadn't thought of before."

"It would mean we'd have to give up our right to make the elves wrong," added Nilrem. "After all, there is a lot of juice in hating the enemy. Hate makes us right. It allows us to dominate others and avoid being responsible for our relationships with them."

"But think of the possibilities for a new way of living," Jake continued. "Peace could replace war as the way of choice. There could be trade between elves and dwarves. Each could learn from the other and prosper in a whole new way."

Nargen, the commander general, stepped to the forefront. "I am the leader of these warriors. All my life, fighting our enemies is all I've known. It is all my father and grandfather before me ever knew. I ask myself, what would I do if there were no more warring? Who would I be then? What would my life then have stood for? Would I have lived in vain?"

"Yes, and what about us?" added a couple of the Longbeards. "All we know is war."

"But consider the costs!" Traylor countered. "Consider the cost in terms of your lives and the lives of your loved ones, the cost to your health. I, for one, am tired of worrying if this night will be my last. I'm tired of worrying how my family will be cared for if I die. Consider the cost in terms of lost relationships with the many good folks who might have been able to contribute to you and you to them."

"Consider again, if the situation were reversed. Put yourself in the little pointed, curled boots of the elves we are about to slaughter!" Nilrem said.

"I see your point," said Yint.

"Me, too," supported Shayli.

The mood was shifting as more and more of the dwarves agreed to look for another way, thinking about what it would be like to be in the other person's world.

"It's settled then," Nilrem said. "I propose we approach the elves in peace, tell them the reason why we need to pass through their village in our search for the Magic Lantern, and ask for their *partnership*! Perhaps we might one day even share the flame of the Magic Lantern with them so that they might have continued peace in their village as well. After all, a lantern loses nothing by sharing its flame with another lantern."

A roar of agreement went up from the crowd.

Nilrem, Traylor and Shayli were voted to represent the dwarves in their request to pass through the elfin village in peace. They approached the elfin leaders cautiously with white flags flying.

To their surprise, they were welcomed with open arms. Their request was gratefully granted by the elves who were equally surprised by the gesture and thrilled for the opportunity to live in peace and avoid bloodshed.

Folo, the elfin leader, personally came to welcome the dwarfen peace party. He was a curious site to behold, dressed in red overalls that were stretched to their limit by a bulging potbelly. With shiny bald head, snow-white beard, ears that protruded prominently at right angles to his round, red face and puffy cheeks that looked like they were concealing chestnuts, one wondered how anyone could consider him to be their enemy.

In a ceremony that brought tears to many a warrior's eyes, Folo presented Nilrem with a beautifully carved tablet that read,

For Life To Work,
Put Yourself In The Other Person's Shoes.

Folo also gave the emissaries of peace the key to the elfin village of Klatsba as a gesture of the newfound friendship between elves and dwarves.

Chapter 4

The Fork in the Road

After two days of celebrating new friendships, drawing up trade agreements, sharing ideas to improve life for all and discussing the many possibilities for future ways that the dwarves and elves might work in harmony together, Nilrem and Jake led the band of dwarves onward, following the path toward Lubidor. The troop was now well rested and in good spirits, high from the experience of what it feels like to make friends and explore possibilities rather than to make war and funeral arrangements.

They traveled on for several days through the valley of Ot in the south, grateful for their auspicious start and cautiously optimistic about what lay ahead.

The Magic Lantern

Jake took advantage of the time he had with Nilrem to ask him some questions about leadership. Nilrem had learned much about what it means to be a leader and was now quite honored to share his insights with Jake.

"Jake, my lord, leadership is a decision one makes to act out of a commitment to a higher good and service to others. All too often, here in Center Earth, as I imagine it is in your world, people confuse leadership with politics. Unfortunately, they couldn't be more different. It seems that the norm has become a situation whereby politicians make decisions that are often ego based, self-serving and reflective of whatever position they see as most convenient at the time. We see all sorts of empty campaign promises with the 'leaders' telling the people whatever they think they want to hear just as long as the rhetoric will get them elected. There's an awful lot of lying, name calling and overall behavior that does not speak well for what leadership really is all about," offered Nilrem.

"It's like that where I come from as well," interjected Jake. "It seems that each side is always looking to take out the other side, make them look bad and show them up in one way or another."

"That's because each side defends their position at all costs," Nilrem continued. "Whenever one person takes up a particular position, it brings up for people the opposite and opposing position. It's like the front of your hand compared to the back of your hand. You can't have one without the other." Nilrem held up his right hand in front of Jake's face turning it to show first the front and then the back side. That seemed to make sense to Jake, but it left him a bit confused.

"But, Nilrem, if people don't take up positions, how do we know what they stand for?" he asked with his face contorted in puzzlement.

Nilrem chuckled. "That's exactly the point! They don't stand for anything. To the contrary, they vacillate on this position today and that position tomorrow, always calling up opposition by someone else who holds a different, often equally valid, position. There is another possibility. That is to stand for a principle or a value without necessarily being attached to a position."

"You mean something like a stand to do the right thing?" said Jake, starting to understand where Nilrem was going with the conversation.

"Exactly right!" retorted Nilrem. "A stand can only be for something, never against something. It's a declaration you make that, by hook or by crook, you're committed to this no matter what. Stands are not based on evidence. A stand is simply a principle or value you support out of a commitment to make a difference in some way. Let me give you an example. Would your folks ever let you starve to death?" Nilrem gave a curious smile followed by his characteristic dwarfen frown.

"Of course not, they love me," Jake responded, without hesitating.

"Exactly," Nilrem said. "Their stand is that, no matter what, as long as they have an ounce of life left in their bodies, they will find a way to make sure that you would not starve. They may not know how. But it's their commitment."

"I see," Jake said. "A stand includes, not excludes. You could say it is a courageous declaration someone makes, creating an opening for possibilities to show up."

"I couldn't have said it better," replied Nilrem with a contented sigh...and frown.

"So let's map this onto our conversation about what leadership is," Jake said.

"Very good. A leader might take a stand for justice, honoring people and doing the right thing —

whatever that means in the moment. And there will be different interpretations about what the 'right thing' is. Nonetheless, how can you argue with a commitment like that? You can't. It's not against anything. Just for things. People. Life. Possibilities," Nilrem said with a passion that underlined each word.

"I can see where, as a leader, by speaking your commitment to some noble idea and actually taking a stand for it, you would put out into the world an energy that serves as a lightning rod to attract possibilities to you that are consistent with your stand," added Jake.

"Yes and beyond that, the courage to take a stand for something will open up a world of new possibilities that might not otherwise become apparent to you." Nilrem could see that Jake was a fast learner. He was excited to have a role in contributing to this up-and-coming leader's development. He continued, "Because a position is exclusive, there is an air of right or wrong associated with it. A position is based on evidence and is usually accompanied by a strong opinion that brings up a contrary opinion, also often based on contrary evidence. People maintaining positions are 'being right' about something and usually unwilling to consider other conflicting positions."

The Magic Lantern

The Fork in the Road

"I can see how positions can lead to divorces, arguments, wars and all sorts of situations that don't support looking for mutuality with others." Jake was really starting to like these leadership discussions.

Nilrem added, "Just like the war we just avoided because we dwarves were willing to give up our position that all elves were our sworn enemies. We had to give up our 'right' to make them wrong, our 'right' to dominate them. When we did and took a stand for peace and possibilities, we found that the elves were willing to give up their longtime position against the dwarfen race as well. Sounds to me like a good first step into leadership for us all!"

Just as Nilrem finished speaking these words, the troop came to a fork in the road. On the right-hand road was a sign that said "The Far Reaches of Lubidor." Lubidor was the dark and foreboding land surrounding Xabor's castle. On the left-hand road was a sign that read "Treasure Mines." Every dwarf knew the Treasure Mines were the caves where pirates of old hid their hoards of indescribable wealth pillaged from their many conquests.

"What luck," Trilion shouted. "This is the road that leads to the riches that are famous in dwarfen legend. I say we take a detour to pursue our fortunes!"

The Magic Lantern

"Why, that could take months, even years," Traylor responded. "Legends tell of dwarves who became lured by tales of hidden treasures only to spend the rest of their lives lost and wandering hopelessly in a labyrinth of caves and passages."

"But think of the gold and the precious gems," added Vester.

And so the dwarves bickered back and forth, divided between those who wanted to pursue the treasure and those who wanted to continue on to their destination as planned.

It was then that Jake stepped forward and spoke. "Oh valiant dwarves, we set upon this journey with a commitment to accomplish a noble mission. That mission is to restore the Magic Lantern to its rightful place in the village square, thus bringing peace to all. Have we lost sight of our vision? Have we lost the focus of our commitment? I entreat you to remember your purpose here on this journey."

Nilrem added, "Lord Jake is correct. We must remember our commitment to peace for all our villagers."

And with those words, the party fell in and followed Jake, Hunter and Nilrem on toward Lubidor. It was on this path that they continued for 23 long and tiring days and nights. It was now the rainy season, and the troop made their journey through constant heavy downpours during 21 of these days. All were soaked to the skin, cranky — even more than is typical for dwarves — and beginning to complain at every turn.

On the morning of the 24th day after leaving the elfin village of Klatsba, the troop came to another fork in the road. On the right again was the familiar sign marking the path to Lubidor. And on the left was a sign that read,

**"Cali's Comfy Cottages —
Wine, Dwarfen Women and Song."**

Upon seeing the sign, a roar went up from the crowd.

"We have to stop."

"How can we pass this by?"

"Count me in."

And a whole lot more of the same type of sentiment was heard in favor of making the detour.

Nilrem turned to Jake and said, "It's never handled! There will always be choices to be made between one's commitment and what seems most convenient at the time." He then turned and addressed the gathering. "Now, fellow dwarves, let us remember our commitment to our objective. We are still a far cry from Lubidor. Every day is important to our people. We must keep to our task of returning the Magic Lantern!"

Grumbling ensued.

"We'll never find a better place to rest a night or two."

"What harm can a little rest and relaxation be?"

"All work and no play make dwarves pretty dull."

In short, Nilrem's pleas fell on deaf ears. The dwarves had had it with the days of rain, lack of sound sleep and soggy, stale bread and seed cakes. The temptation was just too great for them to pass by. Ignoring Nilrem's eloquent words, they turned left toward the cottages.

Chapter 5

The Comfy Cottages

Nilrem continued to plead with the troops to stay the course, but his efforts were to no avail. Jake, too, tried his best to talk some sense into them, but they were not to be denied. So, rather than risk a mutiny, Jake, Hunter, Nilrem, Shayli, Traylor and a few other disciplined souls made camp at the fork while the rest of the group drew lots to see which would be the first group of 10 to visit the cottages. While the rest of the bunch waited their turn at the camp, the lucky 10 proceeded down the hill following the left-hand road in search of the Comfy Cottages.

That evening, when they arrived at the Comfy Cottages, the first group of 10 noticed a sign over the main building that read,

The Magic Lantern

"Enter Here All Ye Dwarves Who Long For Good Food, Drink and Merriment."

"This must be the place!"Vester said with an ear-to-ear grin. He raised his hand and motioned forward, saying, "This way to party time!"

At his invitation, the other nine dwarves followed Vester in. Yint, the last one in, closed the door behind them. As the door slammed shut, the hall went dark, and before you could say "jumping giants," the dwarves found themselves surrounded by a slew of furry arms and legs — all of which were attached to a bunch of smelly trolls.

"Pretty stupid bunch of dwarves I'd say," laughed Jasper, the troll boss. "I can't believe they fell for that old trick!" He stuffed the last of the struggling dwarves into a large hamper used to store hay for the horses. "They'll be some good eatins tanite."

"Yaa, we ain't had roast dwarf in too long," chimed in Harvey, Jasper's second in command.

No matter how much they struggled and squirmed, the trapped dwarves were not able to free themselves. If only they had listened to Jake and Nilrem and not chosen what seemed like a good idea at the time over their commitment to the mission.

The Magic Lantern

Meanwhile, the trolls busied themselves with gathering logs for the fire they would build in the hearth and filling the copper kettle with water from the river in order to boil a nice fat dwarf for gravy. As they went about these chores, their mouths watering at the thought of their succulent dwarf dinner, a gentle breeze carried their telltale troll odor up to the dwarf camp. While the dwarves in camp slept soundly, the troll smell was too strong for Hunter to ignore. As any good hunting dog will, he scurried over to check out the source of the terrible stench. Upon seeing the trolls making their dinner preparations, Hunter returned to camp to waken Jake and the remaining dwarves and alert them to the trouble.

"Why am I not surprised?" Traylor said as he roused the rescue party. "That sign had TROLL written all over it."

"Don't blame yourself, Traylor," Jake comforted. "You did your best to stop them. Let's not waste time bellyaching. We've got work to do."

In a jiffy, Traylor, Shayli and several of the Longbeards and other dwarfen warriors were on their way down to the rescue with a plan.

"One thing we know about trolls," Traylor said, "is that they're greedy."

The Magic Lantern

71

"And not terribly bright," added Shayli.

The warriors quietly approached the cottage where their friends were trapped. Some climbed onto the roof while others hid in the bushes and on either side of the door. When all were in place, Shayli knocked on the door and shouted, "All of the really tasty fat dwarves are out here in case anybody's really hungry!"

The trolls rushed out of the cottage looking to add to their stash with some even better catches. As they did so, the dwarves on the roof lowered their waiting fishing nets onto the unsuspecting trolls. As they tied them up, Traylor led a party into the cottage to rescue the trapped group.

The dwarves emerged from the cottage, grumbling, dusty and smelling of hay but safe and sound. As the sun rose in the morning sky, marking the break of day, they looked over at their former captors to see that they had turned to stone — as trolls will do if exposed to daylight. There they stand today for all to see, stone statues telling a tale of what nearly happened to a bunch of dwarves who chose the path of convenience over the one that honored their commitment.

As Traylor last exited the cottage, he shut the door tight, turned the gold key that was already in the lock and dropped the key in his pocket. As he glanced down at the ground, he noticed a stone with some writing on it. He brushed off the dirt covering it and held it up to the light to see that it said,

Leadership Means Acting From Your Commitment Instead Of What's Convenient.

Chapter 6

The Declaration Stone

S haken but not deterred by their troll experi- ence, the group regained their composure and in unison recommitted to their goal of finding and rescuing the Magic Lantern. As they continued on toward Lubidor, Jake turned to Nilrem and remarked, "I can really appreciate the value of choosing one's commitment over and above what seems convenient at the time."

"Yes, that is certain," offered Nilrem. "The crux of leadership means deciding each and every moment an opportunity for decision arises between standing in your commitment and doing the right thing by taking the 'right' path as opposed to doing what is convenient or taking the easy way out by choosing the other way."

The Magic Lantern

Traylor added, "Also, leadership is often about making a choice between telling the truth versus choosing to look good or to not look bad. It's about doing what's right instead of opting for behavior that you think would cause others to like you. It's about bravely risking instead of playing it safe and small. It's simply a choice between selling out your dream and your commitment to yourself and others or doing whatever it takes to honor it."

"It seems to me that that is what responsibility is really all about," added Jake.

"Most assuredly, my lord, but not in the way that most people view responsibility," countered Nilrem. "Responsibility is really just the ability to respond at any time to any situation in a way that honors you as a person and supports you in your relationships with others. Most people think that responsibility involves blame, burden or fault. And with not being responsible comes shame, guilt or unworthiness. This sort of definition of responsibility really does not support people to be very powerful."

"You mean it's not about how someone *should* do something or how they ought to run their lives?" said Jake, trying to follow Nilrem's drift.

"Precisely," said Nilrem. "Responsibility is really about taking full acceptance for everything that happens in your life. Every event. Every action. Every situation. Because on some level, you have attracted to you exactly what you are experiencing in life."

Nilrem continued, "When you take this point of view that your world is YOUR responsibility, it makes you the source of what goes on around you...not a victim."

"But what about situations that occur that are outside of one's control, like when good dwarves die from a plague or invasion?" Jake said with a perplexed look.

"I am NOT saying that such situations do not take place. They certainly do. Remember, responsibility doesn't involve blame! To say that we are responsible for everything that goes on around us is just a declaration we make that supports us to be in choice," Nilrem continued.

"It sounds like what you're saying is that, by taking responsibility, a leader gives up the 'right' to make others wrong. We realize that we have the power to affect change as the source of everything we attract in the world," Jake said confidently. "Do you know what, Nilrem?"

"What?"

The Magic Lantern

"I have decided to claim responsibility for every-thing that shows up in my life. From there, every day I'll look at what I need to do to impact what shows up around me and, like they say in my world, 'Just do it!'"

"By ghouls and goblins, I think he's got it!" said Nilrem with a broad smile...followed by an automatic frown.

As the troop rounded the bend several miles south of the not-so-comfy cottages, they could hear a com-motion in the distance.

"Ah," Nilrem said with satisfaction. "We are near-ing the fine village of Tsayit. And, Jake, it sounds like our timing is good."

His curiosity now itched for more details, but Jake held his tongue. He could see from Nilrem's face that the sage dwarf had said all he would say for the moment.

As they entered the village, they could see a crowd of several hundred dwarves excitedly gathered round a large glacial boulder. Different dwarves by turn would clamber up to stand squarely on the rock while listening to some comments from the others circled around. Then, after a moment of thought, each pas-sionately recited a phrase to the crowd. This would be followed by a loud and positive ovation from all in attendance.

"What are they doing?" Jake asked.

"I'll let our historian and grand scholar explain this dwarfen ritual to you," Nilrem said, motioning toward Shayli, who made his way forward through the troop to stand next to Jake.

"We call this revered ancient dwarfen ritual 'The Visionary Leadership Profile'," said Shayli. "Twice each year, on the spring and fall equinoxes, all of the dwarves who declare themselves to be leaders take a turn getting feedback from the village. Their fellow villagers tell them what qualities they have that do not support them or may be missing for them to be most effective with others. The villagers also tell them what qualities they see as positively contributing to who the person is in the world. They emphasize characteristics that they would like to see more of in the person. The 'leader' takes in all the feedback silently and with appreciation for the gift of straight feedback. After closely listening to all of the comments, the leader comes up with an invented declaration that embodies all the qualities that his fellows want to see in him," Shayli explained in his signature guttural voice.

"But aren't people afraid to tell their leaders

The Magic Lantern

79

exactly what they see for fear that they will offend them or not by liked by them?" Jake asked.

"Just the opposite," Shayli replied. "The leaders welcome the feedback. We dwarves consider it to be an expression of love given courageously. It's a gift each of us can give to build our friends."

"Sounds like the same sort of decision we discussed before. Folks get to choose if they are more committed to contributing to the person on the hot seat, so to speak, or more concerned with playing it safe, looking good and being liked," offered Jake.

"That's exactly right," Shayli said. "In most cultures, it is typical for people to step over what they really think about other people. The fear is that if I call you on your stuff, you just might call me on mine. It's a sort of unspoken conspiracy."

"You mean it's safer to shut up than talk straight to people," Jake remarked.

"Safer, perhaps," Shayli said, "but clearly NOT in the person's best interests. In this dwarfen ritual, leaders are open to learning all they can about themselves."

Nilrem chimed in, "Much of the feedback comes as a surprise to the person receiving it. We each don't know what we don't know about how we 'land' with others. In many ways, we are blind to how others perceive us. It is in this area that the most personal growth is possible."

"What Nilrem is referring to, we call the three dwarfen realms of knowledge," added Shayli. "What we know. What we don't know. And, most important-ly, what we don't know we don't know. Jake, you know how to speak English. You do not know how to speak Sartic. So, if you got some Sartic books and took some classes on how to speak Sartic, you would then learn Sartic. It would go from the realm of 'what you don't know' to the realm of 'what you do know'. This is how you humans and we dwarves typically make advances. We learn what we don't know, and then it becomes what we do know."

"But these two realms account for only a very small fraction of what there really is to know. The greatest growth comes from reaching the third realm of *'what you don't know you don't know'*," chimed in Nilrem again. "When we can get some insight into this area we are usually blind to discovering, then we are really onto something special."

"So how do we reach this third realm?" Jake asked with interest.

"One way is to get feedback from others," answered Shayli. "That's what the Visionary

Leadership Profile is all about. Here, let's do a couple ourselves. I'll go first if that's all right with everyone."

With the permission of the local Tsayit dwarves, Shayli climbed up on the Declaration Stone, saying,

> *"Hear me now,*
> *Oh dwarfen friends.*
> *Despite all my mortal fears,*
> *I stand before you with open ears.*
> *If you a notion of what may be wrong,*
> *Speak your mind*
> *So that I may try it on!"*

"All right, first, what does not work about Shayli?" Nilrem invited the crowd.

"You're a know-it-all," said Traylor.

"You can be aloof," offered Wert.

"Sometimes, Shayli, you come across arrogantly," added Yint.

"You hide out behind your scholarliness," Jake said.

"You can be afraid to speak your mind at times," added Vester.

"You dress like a boring old dwarf," chuckled Nilrem. "Spruce up your act."

There was a long silence.

The Magic Lantern

The Declaration Stone

"I think that's all for now," Nilrem said. "Now what attributes work for Shayli? And what qualities do you want to see more of in him?"

"You are very kind and generous," Vester said.

"You're brilliant, but you could use more wonderment. Don't have all the answers all the time. It makes others seem stupid around you," Trilion said.

"More humility and authenticity," contributed Jake.

"Vulnerability and sensitivity, let us see your heart, not just your mind," Rilia said.

"You're always there to help. Don't lose that quality. Contribution. We love that about you," added Wert.

"Be more forceful when you speak. Really project your voice," Nargen told him.

"That's great," Nilrem concluded.

"Thank you all so very much for all your honesty, straightness and commitment to my excellence!" Shayli said with a tear in his eye, obviously appreciating the honor of being able to receive such feedback.

Shayli stood firmly on the center of the stone. In a strong, forceful and yet authentic voice, he declared,

"I am a sensitive and caring yet forceful, humbly authentic and vulnerable leader!"

The Magic Lantern

To this declaration, the crowd rose to their feet and let out a loud roar of appreciation.

The leader of Tsayit was Mayor Bluhm. He was a stout old dwarf as wide as he was high. But as a leader, he was 10 feet tall. It was through his inspiration that the Visionary Leadership Profile had become a biannual ritual in Tsayit, making the little village a model for other villages throughout the land to emulate.

With considerable difficulty, the roly-poly mayor, decked out in long white coat and top hat, climbed up on the stone next to Shayli and said before all in attendance, "I present you, Sir Shayli, with this key as a symbol of what it takes to unlock the power inside us all. You are welcome to return to our village to inspire us with your courage and your dwarfen vulnerability at any time!"

"I shall do my best to live from this declaration on a moment by moment basis, knowing full well that the moment I forget to live from my new declaration, I return to a way of being that does not fully support who I choose to be in the world," Shayli said in a voice that emotionally moved everyone in the crowd. "When we live from this new and invented declaration, we then act coming from a place of power simply because we say so. No prior evidence is required.

It is merely a courageous place we stand to maximize our effectiveness with others while being the best we can be in the world."

That day, many other leaders from both the village of Tsayit and the travelers from Mirth stood on the Declaration Stone and received feedback from those they knew and loved. After all were done, they spent the night celebrating each other's courage and toasting their newly re-invented selves.

The next morning, as the troop assembled in preparation to resume their journey, they found a gold key tied to their flag with a red ribbon and bow. With it was a chiseled piece of the Declaration Stone on which was inscribed,

Leaders Have The Courage to Take On A Lifelong Commitment To Personal Development.

Chapter 7

The Caves of Self-Doubt

J ake led the dwarves from Mirth out of Tsayit that morning. Each of them was excited about living their newly invented declarations. It was fortunate that they all decided to immerse themselves in the personal development process since the next challenge they would face would have been the downfall of a group with a lesser commitment.

After two days travel through the blistering desert heat, the troop was parched and in need of a rest when the scouts brought back word of some caves ahead. Now, since the time they are old enough to understand, dwarves are taught by their parents to be very leery of caves. The drier, more livable caves are usually home to evil, squirmy, scaly things that go bump in the night. They have lots of dangerous passages and, as Jake learned all too well, can be fraught with cracks and trap doors that lead to heaven knows where. And at the same time, many caves were cool and comfortable with underground springs that looked awfully appealing to a bunch of tired, hot and thirsty travelers.

As the point dwarf, Traylor led the way as the troop entered the caves to rest for the few midday hours during which the desert sun was the most intolerable. Traylor, Jake and the dwarves made their way toward the spring they discovered at the rear of the cave in search of a cool, refreshing drink. As they sat there talking about how oppressive the midday heat had been and how delicious the cool, clear spring water tasted, they saw a murky fog descending from the ceiling of the cave. Before anyone could see what was happening, the cave was filled with a thick, pea-soup-like cloud that removed all objects from their sight and caused the group to become disoriented and confused.

For hours, through the dense fog, they frantically wandered around in circles, through the maze of passages, unable to find the cave entrance. It was clear to Jake and the dwarves that they had fallen victim to a spell cast by the evil wizard Xabor. This spell resulted in them forgetting who they really were, sending them into a terrible panic. The invented declarations that they had taken such pride in assuming a few days before were now all but forgotten. As they wandered helplessly around in the murky mist, they heard voices sing out,

You're trapped, you're dead, you're out of luck.
You've failed, you've lost, you're in the muck.
Give up all hope,
Your time is done.
You'll never again
See the midday sun.

"We are doomed," Vester said. "We're just not smart enough to find our way out of here."

"We're going to perish here and our mission will have been a failure," cried Yint.

"I knew we should have stayed in our village and not risked our lives for some stupid lantern," moaned Plitor.

"Let's give up. We're going to die anyway," Nargen added.

Jake, too, was despondent. Now he would never

learn the secrets of greatness and return to his own world to make a difference for anyone. He had let his dwarfen friends down, just as he had his parents who wrongly had put their faith in him. What a failure he turned out to be!

As he had these thoughts, he reached into his pocket and discovered the magic amulet that Tonesia had given him in the elfin village.

Jake thought of Tonesia's words to him.

"You have the awesome power to impact the world," she had told him.

In that instant, Jake had a revelation. He did have the power to make a difference. He had it all along. The voices they had heard were merely their own fears echoing through the cave like hollow thoughts through their minds. After all, he knew that fear was just *False Evidence Appearing Real*! How could he have lost sight of this so easily?

Jake rose to his feet, "Hear me now, my dwarfen friends. We do have the power to not only find our way out of these caves but to reclaim the Magic Lantern and bring peace to the village of Mirth — and then, from there to the world. You *are* all capable of greatness. You each can make a difference in your own lives and in the lives of all you meet and beyond — *if you believe you can*! Let us join hands and capes together and take control of our destiny. On the count of three, we'll flap our capes up and down. One, two, three!"

And as they did, as if by magic, the murky fog that had enveloped the cave now lifted.

"There's a stream of light from the outside!" shouted Plitor, pointing in the direction of the cave entrance. "Funny, it was there all along. We just couldn't see it."

"And so it is with all our doubts," said Jake. "We have within us the awesome power to be the magnificent beings that we truly are. If we can only believe in ourselves — that is, truly believe — we will find a way to access that inner strength. As a result, the world will witness our inner power as our actions make a difference for all to see."

"When you believed you could make a difference, new possibilities showed up for you that were previously invisible to you before and the voices of fear and doubt went away," Shayli said.

"What we materialize in life will be directly related to our expectations," added Nilrem.

"If we expect our future to be better than our present condition, we will generate enough self-motivation to do what it takes to realize this expectation."

The Magic Lantern

"Are you saying, we get what we expect?" queried Nargen.

"Most certainly," responded Jake. "From both a positive and negative perspective. When we expect our future to be worse than our current situation, that negative expectation will result in behavior that is consistent with that expectation."

"To say it another way, we sabotage ourselves when we don't believe in ourselves," added Nilrem. "And then we become afraid and act on our fears."

"The Bible, wisest of all man's books, puts it like this, *'As a man thinketh, so he becomes'*," interjected Jake.

"Yes, and if we have an expectation that our future will be about the same as our present state, we will generate an apathetic attitude that will make it be just that — more of the same we have now. We'll generate just enough self-motivation to maintain the status quo. As soon as things are starting to look up, we'll find a way to kick them back to more of what we've been accustomed to expect," Nilrem said.

"It sounds like a built-in thermostat to me," laughed Yint. "The minute things begin to appear promising, if we do not believe we are deserving of them being better, the thermostat kicks us back to our normal state. And if we start to go down hill, we generate just enough self-motivation to get our butts in gear to return to that same old condition to which we are accustomed."

"So, how do we get ourselves out of this vicious cycle?" asked Rilia with a puzzled look.

"That's the $69-million question," smiled Nilrem. "A great leader from the world of men named Richard Brooke tells us the answer is to create a mental vision for what your future will be like. Make your vision so motivating and real that you will expect it to come into being and, as a result of this expectation, do whatever it takes to generate the actions necessary to achieve it."

"You mean we get to create a vision of anything we desire for our lives?" Yint asked.

"Anything and everything that would make life worth living for you," Nilrem said. "You see we all already do have a vision for what our future will look like. For most of us, it's just more of the same that we've had in the past. We use this evidence of past experience to expect more of the same in the future — with some degree of better or slightly different improvements, that is. What we miss seeing is that we can actually create, on purpose, a vision of what our ideal lives will look like. Then it's just a matter of finding what it will take to realize this vision."

"You mean like a plan of action to get there?" Rilia asked.

"Yes, every life decision we make will either bring us closer to realizing our vision or take us further away from it. There's also a magical power that is released in the universe when we actually create a compelling vision and commit to bringing it about in the world," continued Nilrem. "Miracles really do happen!"

"But how do we create such a vision for our lives?" Yint asked.

"There are four main components to a powerful life vision. The first and most important concerns the person you will 'be.' When people speak your name, what qualities will come to mind for them? What will you be known for?" offered Nilrem.

"I want to be known for my courage," answered Nargen.

"For me, it's my wisdom," Shayli said.

"I want others to be inspired by my actions," added Jake. "I want to be an inspiration for people to be and accomplish whatever they dream they can."

"I want to be known as a great humanitarian

among all races — dwarf, elf, human, whatever," Plitor announced.

"Great, you all get the idea. Your vision starts with 'being.' The next question you'll ask yourself is, 'For me to *be* this quality, what would I *do*?' Your actions follow your declaration, that is who you say you are," Nilrem continued. "In other words, if I were this or that, what would I do and how would I think and act?"

"My actions will be bold and courageous," Nargen said, ever the warrior.

"Mine will be wise," added Shayli.

"I would do things that would stretch people to risk and expand who they are. And, most importantly, to believe in themselves," spoke Jake.

"Yes, yes. All of our actions will stem from our being," summarized Nilrem. "Thirdly, what would we *have* as a result of who we *are* and what we *do*?"

"I'd have peace of mind, countless loving friends and all the wealth in the world coming from living the life of a wise and caring friend and leader," Shayli said. As he spoke, a glow emanated from him that brightened the whole cave.

"I'd have a large following of people who themselves would accomplish great things as they were moved by my courage," added Nargen.

The Magic Lantern

"My life will be about leaving a legacy of peace, justice, compassion and abundance for all who are inspired by my example," Jake finished.

"Bravo. Bravo for you all!" Nilrem proclaimed. "You all would have all of the things that come to those who do the things that are in line with the qualities you are being! Notice instead how most folks live life backwards. They mistakenly try to get the wealth, physical and material possessions, the fame, power and glory first. They think that when they get all the things that represent the trophies that life has to offer, then and only then, can they do what they want to do and be the person they want to be. They erroneously look for evidence to prove to them that they are worthy — instead of declaring who they are first and living their lives from this invented declaration. Instead of being, then doing and thus having, they seek to have first. They then wonder why their lives seem so empty and purposeless."

"Yes, certainly that is all very true, Nilrem," said Shayli. "But there is one more element critical to any powerful and inspiring vision. And that is contribution to others. Any vision that is only about you personally is self-serving at best and lacking the inspiration to motivate others to take on your vision themselves."

The Magic Lantern

"Thank you, Shayli. That is so true. It is also the reason why a powerful, compelling vision must be spoken aloud to inspire others. It must live, not just in your head and heart, but in the world for it to have its greatest impact on others," concluded Nilrem. "It is when your vision is clear and compelling and lives as your expectation for what the future holds that it will manifest externally in the world."

As Nilrem finished speaking, the group heard some excited barks coming from the opening to the cave. Jake and the dwarves looked over to see Hunter busily clearing away the dirt that covered a half-buried tablet that had previously gone unnoticed at the cave's entrance. Jake helped Hunter clear away the remaining dirt to see that the tablet read,

We Get What We Expect.

As they removed the tablet, they noticed that beneath it was buried the fourth golden key.

Chapter **8**

The Reflective Pool

The experience in the cave contributed yet another piece to Jake's continuing development as a leader. So very much had happened since he had made that fateful decision to explore the forbidden recesses of the tin mine.

That night, as the dwarves slept, Jake tossed and turned, his mind behaving like a frantic monkey swinging restlessly from one thought to the next. He thought of his mom and dad and worried that they would be frantic about his disappearance by now. He reflected upon the predictable life he had enjoyed on Christmas Mountain and wondered if he would ever get to return to it. He marveled at all of the strange and wonderful things he had discovered in this new and curious world. Could he possibly be King Wiggen come back to fulfill a promise made eons ago after all? Could he actually lead these dwarves to find this lantern of theirs? Would he find a way to make a lasting contribution and a real difference in the world or would he end up dead here in a land that was so unlike his own?

When he could bear the hours of sleeplessness no longer, he got up and whispered to Hunter, "Follow me, boy. Let's take a walk."

Under the light of an eerie full moon, the two headed off in the direction of some massive rock formations not too far off in the distance. They had wandered only a few yards beyond the rocks when they came upon a desert oasis with a broad pool reflecting the moon's glow. With a retriever's inbred love of the water, Hunter rushed in, looking back at Jake as if to say, "Follow me."

As Hunter hit the deeper water, he let out a yelp and charged out just as fast as he had gone in. He rushed up to Jake on shore, grabbed him by the sleeve with his mouth and dragged him down to the water's edge.

As they gazed down into the water, Jake was

startled to see a series of images before him. As he focused more intently on the scene unfolding before their eyes, he realized that he was now watching the living story of his dad's life.

The first scene showed a happy, carefree five-year-old-boy playing with his mom and dad. The little boy obviously felt good about himself and was clearly on top of the world.

In the next scene, Jake watched his dad as a little boy on his first day of school. He watched as the young and frightened little boy, seated at his desk, wet his pants, creating a spectacle for all to see. Merciless teasing by the other kids ensued. Jake just knew instinctively that this was the day that his dad first made up that he was not good enough.

Next, Jake saw images of his dad as a 10-year-old boy. He watched an awkward kid, severely overweight with coke-bottle glasses and an overbite, being tormented by his schoolmates. "Jelly-belly Jil-ian! Jelly-belly Jil-ian!" they repeated in rhythmic cadence. In a few moments, the chant turned into "Pig pile!" as the hooligans jumped on top of the unfortunate little kid in a pile. Jake watched as his dad ran home crying. Jake's eyes were wet, and he felt a sick feeling in the pit of his stomach. He swallowed hard several times before choking out to Hunter, "How can kids be so cruel?"

Jake watched scene after scene, flowing eerily across the pool, in which his dad acted out of this same thought — that he was not worthy and not likeable. He watched his dad fight back in anger and then retreat from people in sadness.

Each time, as a new event reinforced how Chip saw himself, his worthlessness became more and more real until he knew without a doubt that that he was unworthy and not good enough to deserve respect and have friends.

Chip Jilian had started out as a happy, well-adjusted little boy. Then one day, something happened to alter how he saw himself as a person. He decided that there must be something wrong with him, something unlovable. He turned to food to hide the pain. The more he ate to gain comfort the more kids teased him. And, so it continued. The endless cycle generated more pain each time, reinforcing the fact that he really wasn't likeable or good enough after all. The stronger he believed it, the more he brought it about. By eating. By fighting to prove he was tough. And, finally, by giving up and allowing people to treat him poorly.

The Magic Lantern

Now it all made sense to Jake. He understood what had happened to his father and realized that we are *all* guilty of creating this same sort of self-fulfilling prophecy and endless drama cycle to different degrees.

Jake and Hunter walked back to the camp that night in silence.

As he went off to sleep, he whispered to Hunter, "Perhaps this Magic Lantern will shed some light on what we can do to end this vicious cycle of making stuff up so all people can be happier."

Chapter 9

The Listening Shell

What had begun as a quest to return a lantern of peace to a troubled village had now become an exciting, even downright scary, exercise in leadership development for Jake and the dwarfen troop.

As they made their way along their intended trail to Lubidor, the time passed quickly as they spoke of their visions and practiced their invented declarations. Before they knew it, they had left the heat of the desert lands to enter the deep and ancient woods of the Fairytale Forest just as nightfall was approaching.

The Fairytale Forest was long known in dwarfen folklore to be the habitat of a playful race of fairies who took great pleasure in making others happy with their games, tales and jovial nature.

As the dwarves made their way swiftly through the stately trees, they could hear rustling in the branches and the sound of giggling as they went. The giggles soon turned into a catchy little tune that came from the trees above the dwarves' heads.

Listen, oh listen, our little friends.
There's much to do to make amends.
You've marched and worked and learned a ton.
It's time you stopped to have some fun!

So slow your gait
And have a rest,
And learn to listen
To be your best.

Now, dwarves are not the most trusting of creatures. But, nevertheless, the fairies' message was friendly enough to warrant a bit of exploration they thought.

Nargen called the troops together and called out to the fairies, "We come in peace. We are dwarves from Mirth on a noble mission. Show yourselves and be known."

As he finished speaking, hundreds of lighter-than-air fairies swooped down from their hiding places among the tree branches to greet the dwarves and their guest.

Their leader spoke. "Welcome to our forest and be our friends. I am Taldaleen, the fairy princess." Taldaleen had the aura of an angel, dressed all in green with silky yellow hair that flowed to cover diaphanous wings. "What brings you to our enchanted woodlands?"

"We've come from a troubled village called Mirth, just east of the Sartic Mountains, on a noble quest to reclaim the Magic Lantern stolen by the evil sorcerer Xabor. Our journey will end once the lantern we seek is safely returned to the village square and with it, peace and harmony to our people in upset. We have traveled many weeks and have learned many things. We welcome your kind offer of hospitality," Nargen replied.

"By all means," Taldaleen said. "Come and join us for some fresh nuts, berries and a nice bowl of rumbledethumps and share our drink of enchanted ale."

And so they did.

The fairies were splendid hosts. The dwarves, Jake and Hunter sat around the campfire singing fairy songs, feasting on rare forest delicacies and sharing stories of their adventures in search of the lantern.

"Are you always so cordial to your guests?" asked Jake, thoroughly enjoying the experience.

"Why, of course. Are you not the same to your guests as well?" queried Taldaleen.

"Unfortunately, in the world above, we don't always treat strangers with such respect and courtesy," Jake answered honestly. "Especially, when they are different than we are."

"I, too, must confess the same shortcoming with regard to the dwarfen people," conceded Shayli.

"Then, we have much to teach you if you wish to live in peace and harmony, as you say you do," Taldaleen replied. "We fairies were not always so skillful in the art of relationships. At one time in our history, we, too, found ourselves at constant odds with others. Wars were common and discord ruled the forest."

"How did you change things around so dramatically?" Traylor asked with a puzzled look.

"From a far away land to the east came a wise and learned wizard named Tullo."

As she spoke, her words conjured out of thin air a smoky portrait that hung before them. It was the wizard Tullo. He was cloaked in brown with a belt fashioned from rope around his waist. A large hood covered his diminutive head. His long bushy white eyebrows curled beyond the rim of his hood and a long, crooked nose dominated his kind but weathered face. He stood hunched over with the support of a long staff that curled at the top to reveal an orb that lit his way.

"Tullo saw the struggles the fairy people endured and brought with him a gift to present to our people," she continued. With these words, Taldaleen brought forth a large spiral-shaped, coral-and-chestnut-colored shell. "This is the legacy that Tullo left with us. It is called the listening shell."

"What's a listening shell?" interrupted Wert.

"Please allow me to explain," continued Taldaleen. "Before Tullo brought us the listening shell, we all considered, as you most likely do, that everyone's listening is 'empty.' By this, we mean that we listen as though we are a blank slate. To say it another way, when people speak to us, we hear only what they say."

"Yes, is that not so?" Wert interrupted once again.

"It is not," Taldaleen patiently explained. "We all come from different experiences and backgrounds that have contributed to how we listen to others. As a result, we all have an already present way that we listen to others which has been forged from these experiences. The result is that we often do not hear what the person speaking to us is saying at all. What we hear is colored by the filters we have developed over years of occurrences."

"Can you give us some examples?" pleaded Jake.

"Most certainly," Taldaleen said with a smile. " My automatic listening as a leader was 'I already know that.' No matter what the topic, because I not only already knew about what you had to say but also knew more about it than you did, there was very little that you could contribute to me with this listening. To make matters worse, I also listened as to whether I agreed or disagreed with what you had to say. If I agreed with it, I already knew about it and therefore dismissed it. If I disagreed with it, it must not have much merit as an idea, and so I dismissed it as well. The result was that no one could ever tell me anything I didn't know already. My growth was certainly stifled by this listening."

"So how did you fix it?" asked Wert.

"I didn't," replied Taldaleen. "It's not about fixing it. We will always have these automatic listenings to some degree. What there is to do instead is recognize when you are listening in a way that doesn't support your excellence and decide to listen differently."

"So, how do you listen now?" interrupted Wert once again.

Taldaleen brought the listening shell up to her ear. "We all used the listening shell as a sort of training support until we developed our listening skills. My empowered listening, the one I use on purpose, is to listen for the gold in what someone has to say, regardless of their style. When I listen for how someone can contribute to me, I am sure to find a contribution."

"That's wonderful," Jake said. "My automatic listening is for validation. I listen for whether people like or dislike me and also if they agree with me. I guess I take things personally because of this type of listening. So, how can I shift this listening?"

"Here's the listening shell," said Taldaleen, tossing it over to Jake.

Jake held the shell to his ear. "I can listen for people's concerns, their commitments and values. I can also listen for what it's like in their world for them to say what they say. The result will be a greater appreciation for where they are coming from without an interpretation that it's about me personally. Wow, what a relief to give that one up!"

The Magic Lantern

Jake continued, "I can also see that my dad's listening is one of resignation. That looks like, 'What's the use? I'm too old to change. I've tried that before and it didn't work out. So, I might as well give up.' I can see that it would support him to take on listening for possibilities instead. There is always a way fraught with rich possibilities if you listen and look for it on purpose."

"Outstanding!" Taldaleen said. "What's your listening, Wert?"

"That's easy. I listen for brevity. Hurry up and get to the point. If you take too long, I either interrupt or check out mentally. The result is that I miss much that comes from people who speak deliberately and slowly."

Jake tossed the listening shell over to Wert.

Wert held it to his ear and said, "I can listen for the gold as well, knowing that if I hang in there, there will be value for me to get. I can also listen as though there is something valuable at stake both for me and the person speaking. I can see how I will come away from a conversation with a totally different result if I can recognize when I am listening in a manner that doesn't support me or the other person."

"Who else can recognize their automatic listening?" encouraged Taldaleen.

"I can," Plitor said. "I listen to be offended. There is little that people can say that doesn't tick me off."

"No kidding," Yint said. "Your listening has us all walking around on eggshells for fear that we'll say something that might offend you. Do you have any idea of how annoying it is to be around someone with that type of listening?"

Plitor brought the listening shell to his ear. "I will take on listening for the good intentions behind people's speech while listening for what their commitment is to, remembering that it has nothing to do with me personally."

And so, every one of the dwarves took a turn listening through the listening shell. They laughed, shared stories about their listenings and noticed how these affected their lives. All recognized how their automatic listenings didn't support their relationships with others. Each committed to take on listening in a totally new and empowering way. Everyone in the group could not recall when they last spent such an enjoyable and productive night.

In gratitude, the dwarves presented the fairies with several presents which included fine pieces of gem-studded metalwork, stunning pendants and beautifully crafted broaches. In return, the fairies gave Jake and the dwarves the listening shell once presented in similar fashion to them by the wise wizard Tullo. This gift was their most prized possession and the key to their successful relationships. As Nilrem graciously accepted the listening shell and a gold key symbolizing that listening is the "key" to successful relationships, he read the inscription carved on the shell. It simply said,

Whatever You Listen For Shapes Your Reality.

Chapter 10

The Plains of Gatzin

At daybreak, the troop bid their fond farewells to their new friends and set on their quest. Jake breathed deeply and felt fresh energy pulse through him. Everyone stepped briskly through the forest. Hunter bounded ahead, pranced back to Jake, then bounded impulsively ahead again. Emerging from the Fairytale Forest, they had no choice but to venture out onto the Plains of Gatzin on their path to Lubidor.

Emerging from the filtered shade of the lush forest, Jake stopped, aghast. The plains spread bleakly before them. No trees, no mountains. From horizon to horizon, not even a hillock or bush to offer cover. Nargen stopped, too, and pursed his mouth in grim determination. This was goblin land, he knew, where only goblins could find a place to hide. He moved the troops forward, but the band was pitifully exposed for the attack that he knew would come. Brisk steps slowed, swinging arms tensed. More than one dwarf clenched his war club in readiness.

When the attack came, they had only Hunter's sharp, urgent bark to warn them before the masses of nasty goblins swarmed from their underground lairs.

Before the courageous band of seekers knew it, they were completely surrounded by a thousand goblins, slithering and circling around them, cutting off their escape.

As the goblin horde closed in, they chanted,

Who travels here past goblin's fences
Have lost their way if not their senses.
Know you not we hold a grudge?
For murders past
You dwarves we'll judge.

For those who walk the Plains of Gatzin
Will pay the price of wars still lastin'
When poor old goblins lost their souls
As dwarfen hammers took their tolls.

The Magic Lantern

"You judge us wrongly," Jake cried. "We come in peace and ask merely to pass through your land on route to fulfilling our mission to reclaim the Magic Lantern as its rightful owners."

"The young lord speaks the truth," supported Nilrem. "We hold no grudge from dwarfen-goblin wars of past. We seek no confrontation."

We goblins good
Hear dwarfen lies.
We trust you not
For in our eyes
You kill our fathers, sons and daughters
And lead us into dwarfen slaughters!

"Please do not judge us on what happened in the past. We regret the centuries of violence between our people, and we are committed to a new era of dwarfen-goblin peace," Shayli pleaded.

Your words ring false
To goblin ears
For through dwarf hands
Have come great tears
To peaceful souls
In goblin lands.

The Magic Lantern

"Let us prove to you our honorable intentions," offered Nargen, leader of the dwarfen forces. "Upon your word that you will allow us to pass peacefully through your midst, we will lay down our hammers, clubs and cannons until we pass through the Plains Of Gatzin."

After a brief silence, the goblins responded:

Your offer's fair
For wars can't last.
Lay down your arms
And you may pass.

"That seemed too easy. I suggest we proceed with caution," Nargen whispered suspiciously to his troops. "My intuition tells me this is a goblin trick!"

After this whispered warning, though, the dwarf general spoke loudly to his troops so that the goblins could hear.

"Very well, lay down your hammers, clubs and cannons," Nargen instructed his men. "We shall see if the word of goblins can be trusted."

And so the dwarves placed all of their weapons on a goblin cart with the hope that they were not making the last mistake of their lives. As the final weapon was deposited into goblin hands, they heard a shrill cackle echo all around them.

These dwarves are fools
So easily led.
Too bad they soon
Will be quite dead!

And with those words, the treacherous goblin forces surrounded our heroes and prepared to wipe them out in spite of their word given to the contrary.

"Just as I suspected," shouted Nargen above the din. "Not so fast!"

The general reached into his pocket and pulled out a shiny gray cylinder. He reached over his shoulder and launched it amid the heart of the goblin forces. Within seconds, a dense yellow fog covered both dwarves and goblins alike, temporarily blinding goblin eyes. As the goblin forces rolled around on the ground clutching their eyes, the dwarves made haste and scurried out of danger. Not one stopped to look back until they were miles ahead, safe and sound.

When at last the danger had passed, Nilrem turned to Nargen and said, "That was too close for my liking.

But however did you know the goblins could not be trusted?"

"And how did you get us out of there?" added Wert, still panting from the exertion of their flight.

"Well, as we dwarves departed the Fairytale Forest, Taldaleen took me aside. She warned me of the potential dangers to come and gave me the enchanted grenade just in case the dangers she suspected might befall us on the Plains Of Gatzin."

"Then you knew that the goblins couldn't be trusted?" queried Yint.

"I prayed that the goblins might be sincere while preparing for the possibility that they were not," answered Nargen. "Expect the best and be ready for the worst, I say! I could not take a foolhardy chance when the safety of my men was on the line. My intuition told me to be very careful."

"Your intuition is *never* wrong!" confirmed Nilrem.

"Yes. This I have learned. We all must learn to recognize our intuitive instincts and trust them more!" confirmed Nargen.

"But how could those rotten, conniving goblins lie to us as they did?" Vester asked angrily.

Shayli responded, "The goblins did what goblins

do. It's *not* personal. It is wise to assume that *everyone* operates out of the best intentions. They do the best they can with what they know."

"What? How can you say that the goblins had good intentions?" Wert shouted. "They almost had us for supper!"

Nargen continued, "Consider that they did the best that they could do as goblins. Now, I am *not* condoning their actions. They were clearly hideous. But, for a moment, consider yourself being raised as a goblin. You have been told story after story about the treachery of the dwarfen race. You have heard at your grandmother's knee countless tales of the goblin-dwarfen wars and of how innocent goblin women and children have been murdered by the legendary dwarfen goblin-cleavers. Your upbringing tells you that this was yet another dwarfen trick like the hundreds of others you've heard tell. Coming from this perspective, with a commitment to the lives of your people, you did the best you knew how to do. You did the only rational thing a goblin could do operating out of an intention to protect his friends and family."

"That certainly puts things in a different perspective," Rilia sighed. "It almost makes you feel sorry for the goblins."

The Magic Lantern

"Yes. It at least dims your hatred and causes you to think twice before judging them," said Shayli. "Remember the great dwarfen affirmation found in the sacred scrolls, 'Today I shall judge nothing that occurs.'"

"A great ideal to strive to live by," Nilrem agreed.

"Perhaps, another time, they may learn a lesson from some great leader and choose the route of peace instead," Jake wished.

"It sounds like you have already decided to forgive them for what they did," Wert said.

"Yes. There is great power in being able to forgive those you feel have done you wrong," Jake said.

"Those are wise words, my lord," Shayli affirmed. "There is great power in completing with your past and putting it behind you. This is possible only by forgiving. Hatred and resentment are more venomous than the poison of the deadliest serpent. These sentiments consume the spirit and devour the soul. They are far more poisonous to the one hating than the one hated. When you are first to take the initiative to forgive those who have wronged you, you allow happiness to flourish. You transform from a victim to the master of your future, becoming the source of all good things in your life. When you forgive, you unleash the power of miracles. And you release the greatest miracle of all, love."

At that very moment, as they entered the Woods of Lomag, they looked up. Dangling from a tree limb above their heads was a wooden board pierced with an iron spike. A golden key hung from the spike. Written upon the board were the words,

People Operate Out Of Good Intentions — Decide To Forgive.

Chapter 11

Entering Lubidor

The troop had now left behind both their weapons and their desire to wield them against their enemies. They were starting to realize that their enemies were really not much different than they were. Each did the best they could coming from their backgrounds and the way they viewed the world. It seemed far better to understand them, forgive them and help them if at all possible than to hate them, dominate them and kill them.

As they traveled through the Woods of Lomag, the last province of the Land of Possibilities, they readied themselves to enter the Forbidden Land. It was there in that land called Lubidor, that Xabor, the most feared sorcerer in dwarfen legend, lived.

The Magic Lantern

127

The dwarves' long and arduous journey had prepared them well. As Jake and the dwarves stopped to rest and review the six tablets they now carried with them in their sacks, they realized that they now possessed the power to confront whatever evil awaited them. And so, they made ready to penetrate the evil wizard's castle and reclaim the Magic Lantern in the name of peace and harmony for all peoples.

As Jake and his friends crossed the border into Lubidor, they immediately knew that they were no longer in the Land of Endless Possibilities. The terrain had turned barren. The sky was black and filled with the type of menacing storm clouds that portend a violent upheaval to come. The lush woods of Lomag were gone, replaced by tangled and decaying vines and thorny briars. In anticipation of their next meal, angry, squawking vultures circled high above the group, following them as they went.

"Perhaps, we've made a mistake," mumbled Wert. "We can still go back."

"And betray the dream of restoring peace and harmony for all our people?" said Shayli. "Never. I'd rather die trying."

"You speak for us all," encouraged Jake.

"Yes, for us all," repeated all the others, even Wert.

The Magic Lantern

Entering Lubidor

As they crested the hill, the group could now see the foreboding shadow of Xabor's dark and menacing castle just a short distance away. The castle was made of a pitch-black granite not found in the Land of Endless Possibilities. As they approached the drawbridge over the moat filled with hungry alligators, they wished they had not so easily abandoned their swords to the goblin tricksters. The thorns and briars surrounding the moat tore their clothes and pierced their flesh as they inched their way along. After successfully struggling through the bloodying thickets for more than an hour, they at last found themselves at the entrance to the drawbridge. Just as the dwarves set foot on the first rough and splintered plank, the black metal gate blocking the castle entrance abruptly rose. A fierce, green, fire-breathing dragon appeared. The dragon ambled forward and began to make its way toward the troop, spewing forth a stream of fire as it went.

Jake and the dwarves could smell the hair on their arms singe, burned by the intense fire emanating from the dragon's nostrils. With nary a weapon to defend themselves, it appeared that our brave group's journey would soon come to a fiery end.

Jake thought to himself, "This certainly looks like

our darkest hour." He shut his eyes against the dragon flame that would engulf him any moment and clenched his hands until the knuckles cracked. Fear rose thick in his throat like bitter tar.

A sharp pain stung his right hand, rousing him from his paralyzing terror. In his fright, Jake had clutched Tonesia's amulet, and its edges were biting into his palm. The pain cleared his head, and he remembered her words,

"Know that you have the power to make a difference here and always, all your days, no matter where you go. Know also that the love and wisdom you possess deep within your soul is there for you to call upon at will. Now, take this crystal amulet as a reminder of your awesome power to impact the world. Know as well that I will be with you always. You need only call my name in your hour of greatest need."

"Well, this seems to qualify as my hour of greatest need," said Jake aloud. And before he could finish speaking her name, she appeared.

Tonesia was again dressed in flowing white gossamer. She seemed to Jake to be even more beautiful than he had remembered her.

"You're here. You're here. I can't believe you're

here," Jake stammered, regaining a glimmer of hope. "Can you help us? We are at the mercy of this fierce dragon."

Tonesia smiled like a mother consoling her beloved son. "Did I not tell you that I would be with you at all time?" she said.

"Why, yes," confirmed Jake.

"And did I not tell you that you possessed the awesome power of love and wisdom deep within you, ready to be summoned at your beck and call so that you might impact the world?"

"Why, yes. You most certainly did," Jake said, chagrined at the need to be reminded of his power.

"Then, know that the dragon is an illusion that serves you no longer. The sorcerer Xabor has read your mind and tapped into your fears. The dragon is a figment created by Xabor to defend himself from you. He knows no other way to fend off the hurt and pain of his actions. His only weapon now is through intimidation."

Brow furrowed, Jake focused on Tonesia's wise words so fiercely that he never noticed when she faded from sight. He urgently repeated the gist of her message to his friends, and they all suddenly realized that their own fears were their biggest enemy.

The Magic Lantern

"Feel the fear and do it anyway!" Jake said. He turned to face the menacing dragon.

"Now!" he shouted, and he led the dwarves yelling in unison. They charged into the dragon's flames head on and stormed the gate.

By the time that they reached the spot where the dragon had been just moments before, it had vanished, leaving no trace behind, not even a wisp of ash or breath of sulphur. Jake and the dwarves found themselves at the castle's open entrance. Hanging on a peg by the opening was a golden key and a sign that read,

Our Greatest Fear Is Not That We Are Not Powerful Enough, But That We Are Powerful Beyond Measure.

Chapter 12

The Tale of Xabor

Once inside the castle, the troop set their sights on finding the dungeon room. There, according to legend, Xabor had hidden the stolen Magic Lantern. As they made their way through the castle, they saw many inscriptions on the castle walls that seemed to be out of place. These surprised them.

"Look here," Shayli yelled as he pointed to one. It read, *"Without A Vision, The People Perish."* As they went a little further down the great stone hall, Nilrem noticed another, *"There Is No Profession More Noble Than The Fine Art Of Leadership."* And around the corner another, *"The Truth Will Set You Free."* As

The Magic Lantern

they descended the stone stairway leading to the dungeon, yet another, *"There Is No Better Way To Live One's Life Than In Service To One's Fellow Man."*

"Why this is quite perplexing," Nargen said. "Truth, vision, leadership, service. How can an evil sorcerer have such inscriptions on his castle walls?"

As the group rounded the corner, there before them stood Tonesia. Jake could tell by their stunned looks that the dwarves could see her as well as he could.

"Please follow me," she said to the group as she led them into an ancient antechamber paneled in mahogany. Lining three of the chamber's walls were a series of pictures that told a revealing story. A great door faced them on the far wall.

The first picture was that of a handsome young king kneeling beside his beautiful bride, obviously the scene of the happy couple's wedding day. With one finger, Tonesia touched the picture frame while waving her other hand over the group. In that instant the dwarves, Jake and Hunter were transported to the king and queen's wedding day. They hovered above the throng of adoring subjects as formless onlookers, invisible to all below. With wonderment, they watched the following scene unfold:

"Do you, Solas, beloved lord and ruler of the

people, take this woman, Maritsa, to be your queen, to share your reign, from this day forward for as long as you both shall live, until death do you part?" the minister asked.

"I do," said Solas with a smile that landed like fireworks on the crowd.

"And do you, Maritsa, take this man, Solas to be your husband and king, for better or for worse, in sickness and in health, all the days of your life?"

"Yes, I most certainly do," she responded.

"Then, by the power vested in me, I now pronounce you, Solas and Maritsa, king and queen, husband and wife for all eternity. Let no man divide this couple whom God has joined together today. You may kiss the bride, my king."

And with those words, Solas and Maritsa embraced in a long and loving kiss to the shouts and cheers of all who witnessed.

With his arm around his new bride, Solas addressed the crowd, "My loyal subjects, it is with sincere gratitude that I thank you for sharing this, the happiest day of our lives. Today, I pledge to you my commitment to spread this happiness to be the best king that ever lived to rule a kingdom anywhere in Center Earth."

The Magic Lantern

"Long live Solas and Maritsa!" the crowd chanted.

Solas continued, " And I promise you peace, abundance and a lifestyle that will make you the envy of subjects from all other lands. Let us now eat, drink, dance and celebrate this great day!"

The crowd of subjects cheered wildly.

"God bless our king and queen!"

"To the happy couple!"

"Long live King Solas and Queen Maritsa!"

"For they are jolly good fellows!" and the like. It was certainly a day to remember.

Tonesia waved her hand, and in an instant, the troop was back in the antechamber.

"Wow, how did you do that?" Vester asked in amazement, echoing everyone's thoughts.

With a loving smile, Tonesia asked, "What did you get from the ceremony?"

"Solas was on top of the world," Traylor observed.

"His subjects really loved him," Shayli noted.

"He made some pretty serious promises," Yint added.

Tonesia ran her finger to the next picture in line.

In this one, the king was seated upon his throne with his bride seated beside him on hers. Before them were an obviously adoring community of subjects.

Touching this picture, Tonesia waved her hand over the group and they once again found themselves invisibly suspended above the action.

As the king and queen looked out over the adoring crowd, the dwarves heard Maritsa whisper to Solas, "They really do love us!"

"And why wouldn't they? We are the wisest, most benevolent rulers they have ever known," Solas replied with a haughty laugh. "Our people are prosperous. The harvest was again abundant. Life is good. They are in our debt."

Maritsa looked at Solas with a kind and knowing smile, "Now, Solas, my dear, do not lose your humility. We are indeed blessed by the grace of God. Let us not take all the credit for our kingdom's prosperity."

"Nonsense, we deserve the credit! It is through our sound laws and fiscal policies that our people have flourished. I am proud of our accomplishments!"

As Solas spoke these words, Tonesia waved her arm and the group was back in the castle hall.

"Who has an insight?" Tonesia questioned.

Plitor offered, "Solas sure let his good fortune go to his head."

"He thought he could do no wrong," Nargen added.

"He got arrogant," Wert said.

The Magic Lantern

"Very good," Tonesia complimented. "Let us continue to observe the remaining scenes."

The next picture showed the sorrowing king attending his queen's burial. Surrounding him were throngs of mourning subjects come to pay their last respects.

"Must we visit this sad scene too?" Shayli asked of Tonesia.

"If you are to learn and grow in your leadership," she smiled.

"Then take us there," Nilrem pleaded.

With a nod of her head, the band found themselves looking down upon Maritsa's grave.

Solas was beside himself with anger and grief. "Why must this be? My Maritsa! My beloved queen! Where are the doctors responsible for her death? I will have their heads!"

"But my lord, it was not the doctors' fault. It was no one's fault. It was simply the plague," Khor, Solas' chief advisor, said.

"In your kingdom thousands are dying from this same pestilence as we speak," added Watt, the most trusted of the king's council.

"That is no excuse for incompetence! How dare you defy me? Guards, take them away!" Solas lashed out in rage.

The Magic Lantern

"I will host an inquisition into the source of my queen's death and bring those responsible for this plague to justice."

"Enough!" said Tonesia, breaking the spell and returning the troop to the antechamber.

They moved on to view the next picture in the series. In it, they saw an angry mob assembled outside the castle gates. The scene was one of chaos and had all of the earmarks of a revolution in progress.

Tonesia could see that the dwarves from Mirth and their leader, Jake, had been moved by the experiences they just witnessed. "It is important that you observe this last scene," she said.

And with her gesture, off they went to view from their imperceptible perch high above the angry mob storming the castle gates. The ugly scene was marked by desperation. Shouts were heard everywhere and all at once,

"Our children are starving!"

"We need medicine and food!"

"We've lost our cattle, our crops, everything!"

"You promised us abundance. You liar!"

"Come down from your ivory tower and see how your people are dying!"

The Magic Lantern

Tonesia knew that her students had seen enough to prepare them for the lessons to follow. So, back they returned to the castle chamber.

Jake and the dwarves now sought to better comprehend what they had just experienced. "Help us to realize what this all means," Yint asked of Tonesia.

"Let us review the scenes then," she answered.

"The first picture shows the great and benevolent King Solas on his wedding day. King Solas was known as a kind and just ruler and an inspirational leader. He was both much loved by his loyal subjects and looked up to by all who knew him to be a wise and caring leader. The king shared the riches of his kingdom freely with all his subjects and with those of neighboring lands as well. He was known far and wide as a visionary leader and an inspiration for what true leadership can be. His queen was the love of his life and the motivation for this inspirational leadership. Together, they were the much respected and greatly loved leaders of a magnificent and prosperous empire.

"Then one day, a pestilence came to the land, destroying all crops and killing thousands of subjects. It claimed the life of the queen as well. Day after day, the plague spread, taking more lives and killing all animals that the people relied upon for food. Without any crops or animal flesh to sustain them, the people were consumed by a hunger that swept the land. They begged the king to do something. But he was power-less to stop the suffering.

"When the king did nothing to remedy the plague and offered no sustenance, the desperate people revolted. Stricken with grief at the loss of his beloved bride and unable to stem the tide of destruction and suffering, the king lashed out at his subjects.

"He issued an order to behead all who opposed him, the number of which increased with each pass-ing day. The advisors who were unable to provide counsel to get him out of his predicament he consid-ered to have failed him. These he had either killed or exiled from the land. He further demanded that those exiled seek out buried treasure in far away places and not return to him empty-handed, or they, too, would be beheaded. He became known as Xabor, which in the Sartic language means 'he who is without heart.'

"The result was a great reign of terror in which all who surrounded him were either killed or sent away in anger. The once great leader, Solas, had now become the lonely and despised tyrant, Xabor.

The Magic Lantern

"Xabor was consumed with feelings of hatred and revenge. He heard tell of a village where all lived in love and harmony. That village was Mirth. He was furious that there existed such a place of joy when he was so miserable and full of rage. And so, he ordered his trolls to travel to this village and put an end to their bliss. He cast a spell of sleep over the villagers so that the trolls could do their dirty work freely.

"These servant trolls returned with a lantern, which they explained to be the source of the harmony that existed in Mirth. In disgust, Xabor ordered that the lantern be placed in the dungeon room of his castle, hidden under a wooden basket so that the light of love and happiness would never shine on anyone again. He ordered the room be locked with seven sturdy locks and had the seven keys to these locks hidden throughout the neighboring land.

"When word got out of what the king had done, the people hung onto a faint hope that, one day, the keys would be found to unlock the seven locks and thus reclaim the Magic Lantern and the endless possibilities it brought with it. It was thus that the land neighboring the king's land of Lubidor became known as the Land Of Endless Possibilities.

"And so the legend spread throughout the land of

how the Magic Lantern would one day be found and returned to Mirth and its light would shine on all men and women alike, restoring peace, love and harmony to all."

With that, Tonesia concluded her tale and vanished from their sight.

Chapter 13

The Return
of the Magic Lantern

J ake and the dwarves stood speechless for what seemed to be hours outside the door behind which the Magic Lantern was hidden. Finally, Jake motioned to Nilrem saying, "Have someone collect and bring the seven golden keys we have discovered on our historic journey."

In an instant, Shayli appeared, bringing with him all seven keys. Jake picked up the first key. Turning it in the first lock, he repeated,

> *"Put Yourself In The*
> *Other Person's Shoes."*

He next took the second key and, turning it in the second lock, said,

The Magic Lantern

"Leadership Means Acting From Your Commitment Instead Of What's Convenient."

The third key likewise fit perfectly, opening the third lock. As it did, he read,

"Leaders Have The Courage to Take On A Lifelong Commitment To Personal Development."

Placing the fourth key in the next lock in turn, Jake repeated,

"We Get What We Expect."

Next, key number five opened lock number five as Jake spoke,

"Whatever You Listen For Shapes Your Reality."

In similar fashion, lock number six opened with the sixth key. Jake declared,

"People Operate Out Of Good Intentions, Decide To Forgive."

And finally, with much anticipation, the seventh key was inserted in the only remaining lock and, like the rest, opened it with ease. Jake took a deep breath and read,

"Our Greatest Fear Is Not That We Are Not Powerful Enough, But That We Are Powerful Beyond Measure."

Just as the scrolls of old had foretold, the seven magical keys indeed had now been found. After a journey that lasted nearly 14 months and spanned more than 2,000 miles, Jake and the troop of courageous little dwarves at last stood before the unlocked dungeon door. The silence in the room was so heavy that it could have been cut with a knife.

"Our time has come!" Nilrem said solemnly as he reached forward and pushed open the heavy wooden and iron door. As the door creaked open, the dwarves' hearts sank seeing that the room was filled with darkness.

"Why, where's the Magic Lantern?" Wert cried in a voice that did not conceal his grave disappointment.

"Wait, what's that?" asked Rilia, pointing to the far corner of the room.

As the dwarves listened intently, they could hear

The Magic Lantern

quiet sobs coming from the area. As they ventured closer, they saw an old and haggard man, hunched over, kneeling on the floor, with his head in his hands, sobbing and very obviously in great despair.

"Who are you?" asked Nargen.

The old man looked up with a surprised look on his face. "Why, I am, Sol.., er, Xabor, as would be known to the world."

"You are the evil sorcerer of ancient legend?" Jake asked in disbelief.

"Yes, I am the Xabor spoken of in ancient tales."

"What are you doing here grieving on this dark and gloomy dungeon floor?" Yint asked.

"I have made many serious and unforgivable errors in my lifetime. I am both feared and hated by all who know of me. I grieve for the sins of righteous anger and hatred committed by a confused man many centuries ago," Xabor said solemnly.

"But what of the Magic Lantern?" Shayli demanded. "Did you not steal it from the village of Mirth and is the lantern not here in your possession, as told by legends of old?"

"Yes, indeed, I ordered the lantern to be removed from the village square. My grief for the loss of my beloved bride and of the respect of my once loyal subjects was simply too great for me to bear. I sent for the lantern but refused to look upon it. I ordered the flame to be extinguished so that the light of love and happiness could never be felt by anyone else. With this, I had hoped to gain comfort by having others share in my misery," Xabor sobbed.

"Did it work? Did it make you feel better?" asked Trilion.

"No, it did not," Xabor answered. "As word returned to me of the suffering, unhappiness and upset rampant throughout the land, I hated myself more and more. But, alas, I was resigned that what I had done could not be reversed."

As he spoke, Jake noticed a mound covered by a heavy cloth in the other corner of the room. "What is that?" he asked.

"I know not," Xabor said, with a shrug.

Jake walked over to the mound. The tarp was thickly layered with the dust of many years. He removed the tarp and found beneath it a heavy wooded bushel basket. He motioned to Nilrem for assistance in lifting the heavy basket. As they did, a brilliant light, brighter than any they had ever witnessed, flooded the room, causing Jake, Xabor and the dwarves to recoil in surprise.

The Magic Lantern

"The Magic Lantern!" shouted Shayli. "It is here and burns as brightly as ever after all!"

Jake went over to the golden lantern, picking it up to examine it more closely. As he lifted it high, he noticed a dusty inscription etched on its base. The inscription read,

The key to an unending life of bliss
Lies here before you, too simple to miss.
For the light of the lamp
To never extinguish,
Its facts from interpretations
You must learn to distinguish!

As Jake finished reading the inscription, Tonesia appeared in a brilliant flash of white light of her own.

She smiled a loving smile and with a wise and knowing look she explained, "Listen carefully. The key to happiness is given. The lantern's message is clear. If you wish to lead lives free of upset and filled with warm, loving relationships, you must become adept at separating facts from interpretations. The source of disharmony in the world is that we all listen to others and then make things up that cause us to go into our moods. Each person's own particular mood is one of either anger, fear or sadness. When someone says or does something, we make things up about what was said and done that lands us squarely in this mood. We mistakenly confuse what happened or what was said with an interpretation we create, resulting in this mood. Our interpretations are not true. We just make up that they are because these interpretations make us angry, sad or afraid."

"But who wants to be angry, sad or afraid?" asked Nargen.

"Our moods are familiar and addictive, more so than the strongest poppies," Tonesia continued. "We say we don't want to be angry, sad or afraid, but we are helpless to rid ourselves of these addictive moods. For there is a huge payoff that results from getting into your mood. Your mood allows you to be right! It makes you better than other people. It allows you to dominate them and keeps you from being hurt by them. It removes your responsibility to be in relationship with others and make life work. Instead you can simply be mad at them, or afraid of them or sad at what they did or said. Your mood allows you to feel sorry for yourself. It makes you a victim. After all, who can blame you for being angry, sad or fearful? It was not your fault! You're entitled to your feelings! Or at least, that's the story you sell yourself."

The Magic Lantern

"But how can we get out of our moods?" Rilia asked her.

"By separating the facts from the interpretations that land you in your mood!" Tonesia responded. "The key is to first recognize your most familiar mood."

"Mine is sadness," offered Shayli. "I scan for interpretations that will make me sad. I don't really want to be sad, but it seems like I am helpless to prevent it as all of life's events and people's words seem to make me sad."

"It's not the words or the events that make you sad, it's the interpretations you make up about them that does!" Tonesia interrupted. "When was the last time you remember being in your sad mood?"

"Why, just moments ago," responded Shayli. "I was depressed when it appeared that the Magic Lantern was not to be found here."

"Let's separate what happened from what you made up about it," continued the good white wizardess.

"What happened was Xabor said, 'I ordered the flame of the Magic Lantern to be extinguished'," said Shayli.

"And what interpretation did you make up about

what he said that landed you in your mood, causing you to be sad?" she prodded.

"I made up that all hope was lost without the lantern. People would always be in upset. And that made me sad."

"Good. Now what other interpretation could you have made up that would be empowering instead and not land you in your mood?" she continued.

"I could have made up that Xabor was mistaken. That the lantern was still to be found. Or I could have made up that people could live in love and happiness without the lantern if they were committed to this, or I could have made up that there must be another way to bring happiness to the world, or..."

"That's quite enough empowering interpretations to give us all a good idea of how it's done," interrupted Tonesia. "Notice that each of the empowering interpretations did not have a mood attached to it for you. For that reason, these interpretations may have seemed kind of strange or felt not just right. There was no mood associated with them. But, just as you made up the interpretation that sent you into your mood, you have the power to make up a new one that does not."

"Wow!" Wert said. "When Xabor said whatever it

was he said, I became righteously angry. I made up that he had one heck of a nerve to extinguish the flame, after all we did to get here!"

"So, your familiar mood is anger?" she asked Wert.

"Not just plain old anger, but righteous, indignant anger," smiled Wert, followed by a frown. "I live in that mood. I feel it all the time as heat in my face and a shaking in my body."

"And your new, invented interpretation?" asked Tonesia.

"That's easy. It's that I've learned so very much on this journey and that I'm not the man I was when I started it. Even if there was no lantern, the trip was incredibly worthwhile. Really, it was life changing!"

"Wonderful," smiled Tonesia. "There's no mood attached to that one. What about you, Yint?"

"Well, when I heard Xabor say that, I became scared. What would happen to us all now if there was no longer a remaining flame? I thought we'd all surely perish. I clearly made it up."

"And your new interpretation?"

"That no matter what, we'll find a way to be safe and happy."

"There really is a magical power in this tool that the lantern offers us!" Jake said excitedly. "So, what

The Magic Lantern

about you, Xabor? When the plague came and your wife died, what did you make up about it?"

Xabor picked himself up off the floor. "Well, I can see now that the facts were first, a plague came and second, my wife died. And what I made up about it was that I must be a pretty stupid ruler to allow this to happen to my people and especially to my dear beloved wife. I felt humiliated."

"And you couldn't handle being stupid?" offered Jake sympathetically.

"Not only could I not handle it, but it made me furious at myself! I just turned this inner rage outwardly toward others. You see my familiar mood is raging anger followed by resigned sadness. And, of course, my actions of killing and exiling those who opposed me made me just angrier and sadder! And now I see that I could just as easily make up that plagues and pestilence are part of life. They were not my fault. I was not stupid. I did the best I knew how to do to keep my people safe."

Xabor continued, "But what I have done was terrible! I brought death and suffering to millions. How can I ever undo all of the misery I have created? I am truly, truly sorry for what I did."

Jake looked at the once powerful king with

compassion. "Would you be willing to start by forgiving yourself first?" Jaked asked him. "I see that you made some terrible mistakes and we certainly do not condone your actions. However, as I see it, you have two obvious options. You can waste away in sorrowful pity here in your dungeon or you can recognize the error of your ways and commit to doing some good in the world."

"I am willing to commit to spending my every remaining day in pursuit of good and committed to relieving suffering in the world," Xabor told him. "I shall journey with any and all who will join me to bring the light of the Magic Lantern along with its message of hope — that is, how to live a life free of upset — to every village and every land starting with the Land Of Endless Possibilities."

As he spoke these words, years of age and pain were instantly erased from his face.

"Let us again call you Solas, as you were once called before. I forgive you and feel that many others will as well. What's more, I will join you in your quest to spread the lantern's light and message of hope to all," Shayli said.

"As will I," said Nilrem. Then Nargen agreed. Then Rilia. And so likewise spoke every last dwarf inspired by Solas' vision.

The Magic Lantern

The Return of the Magic Lantern

Chapter **14**

The Legacy of Solas and the Dwarves of Mirth

T rue to their word, the dwarves accompanied Solas throughout the lands, lighting a new Magic Lantern and spreading its message of hope and love in each area they visited.

From this initial group of about 30 leaders, millions of others learned the lantern's message and were inspired by it to step into leadership of their own. The result was that in each town and village, wood and cave, inhabited and remote area, leaders were developed who followed the seven key principles as taught by the tablets.

Solas became known far and wide for his love of others and his commitment to peace and excellence for all. After many, many years of living these values,

The Legacy of Solas and the Dwarves of Mirth

Solas was relieved to see that the ancient stories of an evil sorcerer became obscure and largely forgotten. In sharp contrast to these old tales of horror, the new legends spoke of a kind and compassionate leader and servant committed to the well-being of all.

As a result of the work of Solas, the dwarves of Mirth and the leaders that sprung up all around them, the lands of Center Earth experienced a renaissance period of 10,000 years in which peace, love and a commitment to "do the right thing leadership" dominated the world.

As for Jake, he triumphantly returned to Mirth with the dwarves returning the Magic Lantern to the village square. Just as it had once before, it would now again cast its glow of peace. Upon the lantern's return, the villagers implemented its message, and all fighting and upset stopped. Talk of war was replaced with talk of contribution to others. The villagers from Mirth celebrated the return of their courageous and heroic men with a parade of grand proportions. Holding the Magic Lantern high for all to see, the dwarves traveled along every street of the village, allowing it to cast its mood-altering light of harmony on everyone it touched. What had been for too long the village of Constant Upset was truly, once again, the village of Mirth.

The Magic Lantern

The Legacy of Solas and the Dwarves of Mirth

Jake rejoiced in the role he had played leading the dwarves to find and return the Magic Lantern. But equally important to all was the process of personal development and empowerment that everyone experienced along the way. None of the travelers were now, at journey's end, the same people they had been when the whole quest all had begun some 14 months before.

Now, as the parade approached the village square where the Magic Lantern would be hung for all eternity to cast its harmonizing glow, the villagers paused to honor the brave young man from the world above who had contributed so much to the successful quest. Nilrem, Shayli and the rest of the dwarves gathered round their friend, Jake, who now stood directly beneath the lantern's glow.

In a ceremony that called up all of the pomp and respect that dwarves have to offer, the villagers of Mirth honored Jake as their hero. As men, women and children cheered and cried tears of joy, Nilrem stepped forth and said, "Lord Jake, it is with heartfelt gratitude and love that we present you with this token of our affection and appreciation."

With these words, he presented Jake with a hand-crafted solid gold lighter in the shape of a lantern. The lighter was inscribed with the words of wisdom found on each of the seven tablets. With tears in his eyes and a lump in his throat, Jake climbed up the tall wooden ladder leaning against the lamp post and lit the lighter's flame with that of the Magic Lantern. He accepted the magnificent present, saying, "My dearest friends, I thank each one of you for your friendship, partnership, inspiration and courage. I shall remember your contribution to my life and to the lives of countless others for as long as I shall live. I love you all very much and will never forget you!"

As he spoke these words, the villagers cheered wildly. Many gathered around the ladder, wanting to shake his hand and personally thank him for his great courage in leading the expedition. As the villagers closed in on Jake, several brushed against the ladder. Before anyone could stop the ladder from falling, it crashed to the ground with a terrible thud. Amidst the crowd of excited dwarves gathered there in a heap, Jake lay unconscious at the bottom of the pile.

Chapter 15

The World of Men

When Jake regained consciousness, he found himself looking up at Hunter, his faithful dog, who was excitedly licking his face. There were voices all around him, and Jake became startled as someone shown a bright light in his eyes.

"It must be the Magic Lantern," he thought, shielding his eyes from the glare.

"We thought that we had lost you for a moment," said a concerned voice. He recognized it as his dad's.

"Where am I? What happened?" Jake asked. Still dazed, he was not expecting to see his father. And where were all his dwarf friends?

The Magic Lantern

"Hunter came to get us. You must have fallen and hit your head on a rock as you explored that old, abandoned mine passage," Jake's mom said as she applied a cold towel to the lump on Jake's forehead. "It's a good thing we had your cave wall writings to follow to find you."

Hunter let out a yelp as if to remind them, "What about my help!"

"Yes, and if it were not for Hunter, we never would have found you," Chip said with a stern tone of concern in his voice.

"Why, I've had the most incredible experience," Jake tried to explain. He was beginning to realize that while he had been exploring Center Earth for 14 months, no time had passed in the lands above.

"We can see you have!" Sarah replied, sarcasm lacing the relief in her voice. "Let's get you out of here and you can tell us all about it."

As they made their way out of the mine, through the passages of the cave and finally into the bright afternoon sunshine, Jake reached into his pocket. He pulled out a crystal amulet, a beautiful gold lighter and a crumpled piece of paper.

Jake unfolded the paper and read its message, "I am an inspirational, charismatic leader who, through love and wisdom, will bring peace and understanding to the world." He recognized it to be his invented declaration drafted that day in Tsayit.

Chapter 16

Epilog

J ake returned to his life on Christmas Mountain that day, trying to explain to everyone how the amulet, lighter, and the paper with his invented declaration had gotten into his pocket. He recounted the entire tale of how he and his dwarfen friends had journeyed throughout the Lands of Endless Possibilities and Lubidor on their quest to return the Magic Lantern to the village of Mirth. Jake's mom, dad and friends dismissed his tale as the vivid dream of a 15-year-old boy who had suffered a blow to the head. Despite their disbelief, no one could explain just how Jake could gather so much wisdom about leadership, personal effectiveness and relationships apparently overnight. They simply attributed it to Jake applying

The Magic Lantern

himself to learn about such things in books and in school.

From that day forward, Jake lived each day out of his newly invented declaration. He worked tirelessly with his dad, Chip, helping him separate facts from interpretations. Through this work, Chip came to better appreciate how he saw the world. He also saw how many of the interpretations that he had made up did not support his happiness and his relationships with others. Apparently, Chip's mom had been obliged to get a job starting when Chip was just six years old. As a six-year-old, Chip had made up that she must not love him very much since she chose to work instead of opting to be with him when he returned home from school each day. He also made up that he was not worthy of her love. Jake had helped him to see that the facts were simply that his mom had worked. What he had made up was that he was not good enough and that his mom didn't love him. In place of this interpretation, Chip was now willing to create a new interpretation that his mom loved him so much that she went to work to better provide for him even though she would have rather stayed at home with him. He was more than just good enough. He was her pride and joy!

The Magic Lantern

Epilog

Chip, or rather Jim, as he now chose to be called, gave up his attachment to his moods of pitiful anger and resigned sadness on that very day. His new interpretations supported him in repairing many of the relationships he had sabotaged while in his mood. Daily, people commented on their observation that Jake's dad no longer appeared to have that chip on his shoulder. He shaved, lost 120 pounds and started to hold himself differently — as a person worthy of respect and love. In fact, just about everyone Jake touched seemed to be more effective with people and displayed a greater gusto for living.

Jake never forgot the lessons he had learned in the lands of Center Earth. As he grew up, he took on the challenge of realizing his vision for world peace. He took a stand for the excellence of others and was an inspiration to millions who followed his leadership. At the age of 30, Jake became the youngest U.S. Senator to hail from the state of New Hampshire. He was responsible for numerous political reforms and he redefined what leadership in America was really all about.

At the age of 35, Jake was elected as the youngest President of the United States of America. During his two terms in office, he set a new standard for excellence and harmony in relationships between all countries and their peoples. Perhaps President Jilian's greatest accomplishment was in helping countries create empowering interpretations that support peace instead of war. In fact, during his eight years in office, Jake saw to it that the Magic Lantern burned brightly in every country in the world. It marked the first time in the history of mankind that war was nonexistent on the planet. History went on to mark the Jilian presidency as the start of a thousand-year era of peace on earth.

When asked how he could have so effectively spread peace from country to country and individual to individual, Jake simply answered, " A lantern loses nothing by sharing its flame with another lantern. Please don't hide your light under a basket. Share its glow with all you meet."

And that is exactly what everyone did! And that is why this is only THE BEGINNING.

The Magic Lantern

About the Author

Dr. Joe Rubino is widely acknowledged as one of North America's foremost success and productivity coaches. He is the CEO of Visionary International Partnerships. To date more than 100,000 people have benefited from his coaching and leadership development training. Together with Dr. Tom Ventullo, he is the co-founder of the Center For Personal Reinvention, an organization that provides coaching, productivity and leadership development courses that champion people to maximize their productivity, personal power and effectiveness with others.

He is the author of three additional books including, *The Power To Succeed — 30 Principles For Maximizing Your Personal Effectiveness, Book I*; *The Power To Succeed — More Principles For Powerful Living, Book II* and *Secrets of Building A Million Dollar Network Marketing Organization From A Guy Who's Been There Done That and Shows You How To Do It Too.*

To request information about any of the Center For Personal Reinvention's programs or to order any of Dr. Rubino's books, visit http://www.CenterForPersonalReinvention.com.

Dr. Rubino can be reached via Email at: drjrubino@email.com. or Fax: (630)982-2134.

The Magic Lantern

The Center For Personal Reinvention
Dr. Joe Rubino and Dr. Tom Ventullo

Where are you stopped in your life and in your business?
Where is there an unacceptable level of resignation or conflict?
Where are there interpersonal listening and communications skills lacking?
Where is there a missing in terms of partnership, commitment and vision?

The world we live and work in is marked by unprecedented change and fraught with new and complex challenges. For many of us, life begins to look like an uphill struggle to survive instead of a fun and exciting opportunity to grow, risk, and play full out in partnership with others. The stresses, conflicts and frustrations we experience daily need not be so.

In place of these, there exists another possibility.

...To live and work in choice - empowered by the challenges of life.
...To champion others to achieve excellence in a nurturing environment that fosters partnerships.
...To acquire the success distinctions that support mutuality, creativity and harmony.
...To take on the art of listening and communicating in such a way that others are impacted to see new possibilities for accomplishment, partnership and excellence.

Reinventing ourselves, our relationships and our perception of the world is the result of a never ending commitment to our own personal magnificence and to that of others. It is made possible through the acquisition of approximately fifty key principles that cause people to begin to view life and people in an entirely different way. When people really *get* these principles, the quality of life and relationships improve and new possibilities for breakthroughs show up. Through the use of cutting edge technology as a vibrant basis for learning, growing and acting, *The Center For*

The Magic Lantern

Personal Reinvention is successful in shifting how life shows up for people by supporting them to self-discover these life-changing principles.

With this program, YOU will:

- Uncover the secrets to accessing your personal power while maximizing your productivity.
- Gain clarity on exactly what it will take to reach your goals with velocity.
- Create a structure for skyrocketing your effectiveness while developing new and empowering partnerships.
- Learn how taking total responsibility for every aspect of your life and business can result in breakthrough performance.
- Discover what the key elements are to a detailed action plan and how to reach your goals in record time.
- Acquire the keys to listening and communicating effectively and intentionally.
- Recognize and shift out of self-defeating thoughts and actions.
- Gain the insight to better understand others with new compassion and clarity.
- Learn how to develop the charisma necessary to attract others to you.
- Experience the confidence and inner peace that comes from stepping into leadership.

The Center For Personal Reinvention

...Bringing people and companies back to life!

Customized Courses and Programs Personally Designed For Achieving Maximum Results

Areas of Focus include:

Designing Your Future
Making Life and Businesses Work
Generating Infinite Possibilities
Creating Conversations For Mutuality
Commitment Management
Personal Coaching and Development
Maximizing Personal Effectiveness
Breakthrough Productivity
Leadership Development
Relationship and Team Building
Conflict Resolution
Listening For Solutions
Systems For Personal Empowerment
Personal and Productivity Transformation
Designing Structures For Accomplishment
Creating Empowered Listenings
Possibility Thinking
Forwarding Action
Structures For Team Accountability
Innovative Thinking
Completing With The Past
Creating A Life Of No Regrets

The Center For Personal Reinvention champions companies and individuals to achieve their potential through customized programs addressing specific needs consistent with their vision for the future.

Contact us today to explore how we might impact your world!

The Center For Personal Reinvention
PO Box 217,
Boxford, MA 01921

drjrubino@email.com
Fax: (630) 982-2134

The Magic Lantern

Other Books By Dr. Joe Rubino

The Power To Succeed:
30 Principles For Maximizing Your Personal Effectiveness

What exactly distinguishes those who are effective in their relationships, productive in business and happy, powerful and successful in their approach to life from those who struggle, suffer and fail? That is the key question that *The Power to Succeed: 30 Principles For Maximizing Your Personal Effectiveness, Book I* supports readers to explore in life-changing detail. The information, examples, experiences and detailed exercises offered will produce life altering insights for readers who examine who they *are being* on a moment to moment basis that either contributes to increasing their personal effectiveness, happiness and power — or not. As you commit to an inquiry around what it takes to access your personal power, you will gain the tools to overcome any challenges or limiting thoughts and behavior and discover exactly what it means to be the best you can be.

The principles that renowned productivity coach, speaker and trainer, Dr. Joe Rubino discusses in this book are responsible for transforming his own life. Dr. Rubino is a retired dentist who changed careers at the age of 37 to devote his life to assisting others to be more effective in their relationships and happier and more productive in their lives. Dr. Rubino's commitment is to now share the same principles that transformed his own life with others so that they too might maximize their personal power and effectiveness.

With this book YOU will:
- Uncover the secrets to accessing your personal power.
- Create a structure for maximizing your effectiveness with others.
- Learn to take total responsibility for everything in your life.

The Magic Lantern

- Discover the key elements to accomplishment and how to reach your goals in record time.
- Identify your life rules and discover how honoring your core values can help you maximize productivity.
- Complete your past and design your future on purpose.
- Discover the keys to communicating effectively and intentionally.
- Stop complaining and start doing.
- Seize your personal power and conquer resignation in your life.
- Learn how to generate conversations that uncover new possibilities.
- See how embracing problems can lead to positive breakthroughs in life.
- Leave others whole while realizing the power of telling the truth.
- Learn how to develop the charisma necessary to attract others to you.

———— ❦ ————

The Power To Succeed: More Principles For Powerful Living, Book II

This revealing book continues where *The Power To Succeed: 30 Principles For Maximizing Your Personal Effectiveness, Book I* left off with more powerful insights into what it takes to be most happy, successful and effective with others.

With this book YOU will:
- Discover the keys to unlock the door to success and happiness.
- Learn how your listening determines what you attract to you.
- And how to shift your listening to access your personal power.
- See how creating a clear intention can cause miracles to show up around you.
- Learn the secrets to making powerful requests to get what you want from others.
- Discover how to fully connect with and champion others to realize their greatness.

The Magic Lantern

- Learn to create interpretations that support your excellence and avoid those that keep you small.
- Develop the power to speak and act from your commitments.
- See how communication with others can eliminate unwanted conditions from your life.
- Discover the secret to being happy and eliminating daily upsets.
- Learn how to put an end to gossip and stop giving away your power.
- Develop the ability to lead your life with direction and purpose and discover what it's costing you not to do so.
- And More!!

The Power To Succeed: 30 Principles For Maximizing Your Personal Effectiveness, Book I and its sequel, *The Power To Succeed: More Principles For Powerful Living, Book II* are a powerful course in becoming the person you wish to be. Read these books, take on the success principles discussed and watch your life and business transform and flourish.

Have you read the best selling book that can teach you everything you need to know about how to build a successful network marketing empire?

"SECRETS OF BUILDING A MILLION DOLLAR NETWORK MARKETING ORGANIZATION FROM A GUY WHO'S BEEN THERE DONE THAT AND SHOWS YOU HOW TO DO IT, TOO."
By Dr. Joe Rubino

Learn the Keys to Success in Building Your Network Marketing Business - From the Man Success Magazine called a "Millionaire Maker" in their December 95 Cover Story.

The Magic Lantern

With This Book You Will:
- Get the 6 keys that unlock the door to success in MLM.
- Learn how to build your business free from doubt and fear.
- Discover how the way you listen has limited your success. And ...
- Accomplish your goals in record time by shifting your listening.
- Use the Zen of Prospecting to draw people to you like a magnet.
- Build rapport and find your prospect's hot buttons instantly.
- Pick the perfect prospecting approach for you.
- Turn any prospect's objection into the very reason they join.
- Identify your most productive prospecting sources. And ...
- Win the numbers game of network marketing.
- Develop a step-by-step business plan that ensures your future.
- Design a Single Daily Action that increases your income 10 times.
- Rate yourself as a top sponsor and business partner.
- Create a passionate vision that guarantees your success. And More!!!

"This is perhaps the best book available today on how to build a network marketing business."

— John Fogg,
Founder of *Upline®* Magazine

"Joe's book is the bible on how to build a successful MLM business. I suggest — as persuasively and powerfully as I can — that you take on mastering Network Marketing the way Dr. Joe Rubino has.

Don't just read this book- devour it!

— Richard Brooke
Author, *Mach II With Your Hair On Fire*

**LEARN WHAT IT TAKES
TO BE AT THE TOP IN YOUR COMPANY!**

The Magic Lantern